Mani Singh Basi is a barrister at 4PB. He is a practitioner who has a specialist interest in cases with an international element. As such, he regularly appears in the High Court in cases relating to the inherent jurisdiction of the High Court such as child abduction. He was the winner of the Family Law Commentator of the Year Award at the LexisNexis 2022 Family Law Awards and previously published a book titled 'A practical guide to stranded spouses in family law'. In 2023, he was shortlisted for the International Lawyer of the Year award.

A Practical Guide to Exercising the Inherent Jurisdiction in Family Law Proceedings

A Practical Guide to Exercising the Inherent Jurisdiction in Family Law Proceedings

Mani Singh Basi

Law Brief Publishing

Published 2023 by Law Brief Publishing, an imprint of Law Brief Publishing Ltd
30 The Parks
Minehead
Somerset
TA24 8BT

www.lawbriefpublishing.com

Paperback: 978-1-916698-20-8

PREFACE

The inherent jurisdiction is a powerful tool to ensure that children subject to proceedings are properly protected, which can be achieved in a number of different ways. The inherent jurisdiction is often regarded as a complex area of family law due to the complexity of cases that enter its arena, ranging from child abduction disputes and determination of cross-border issues, wide-ranging injunctive powers, orders relating to medical treatment and disputes relating to challenging public and private law proceedings.

This book will provide practitioners working in family law with a toolkit as to how to embark upon proceedings relating to the inherent jurisdiction. There will be a focus on the types of orders that can be made under the inherent jurisdiction and consideration as to the purpose. The book will consider the inherent jurisdiction across a range of different practice areas within family law, such as child abduction, private and public law disputes and other injunctive/protective orders that are designed to safeguard children. In particular, this book will consider in the context of the inherent jurisdiction: tracing/locating children and respondents, deprivation of liberty, forced marriage protection orders, female genital mutilation orders, inward and outward abduction, vaccinations, tipstaff orders, and disputes relating to medical treatment. This book will consider the limits to the inherent jurisdiction as well as how practitioners can best present cases in terms of case management from the outset of proceedings all the way to the conclusion of proceedings, whether you are acting for an applicant, respondent, the subject children or any other interested party within proceedings.

The law is accurate as of 1st September 2023.

Mani Singh Basi
September 2023

CONTENTS

CHAPTER ONE

AN INTRODUCTION TO THE INHERENT JURISDICTION

Introduction

This chapter will focus on what is meant by the inherent jurisdiction. The definition has been subject to much debate over the years in the High Court and even at a lower level in the family court. The inherent jurisdiction is debated in terms of what limitations exist in respect of the powers that the court can exercise. As such, there is a vast amount of case law that provides guidance on what the inherent jurisdiction can be used for and once it is engaged, its limits, if any, in order to protect children.

The inherent jurisdiction is a special term that is fairly unique to England and Wales, not in respect of its existence, but in the manner that it is ultimately utilised. It must however be acknowledged that a number of other countries do have an inherent jurisdiction, such as Canada, Australia and the United States. Notwithstanding this, it is England and Wales that have attracted a lot of attention in respect of their use of the inherent jurisdiction, because the inherent jurisdiction has proved to be a very creative tool in many different avenues relating to child protection, as this book will consider.

The inherent jurisdiction

All the way back in 1968, Lord Denning in Re L (An Infant)[1] stated in respect of the inherent jurisdiction:

---

1 [1968] P 119, para 156

> *"It derives from the right and duty of the Crown as parens patriae to take care of those who are not able to take care of themselves. The Crown delegated this power to the Lord Chancellor, who exercised it in his Court of Chancery. ... the Court of Chancery had power to interfere for the protection of the infant by making whatever order might be appropriate. ... This wide jurisdiction of the old Court of Chancery is now vested in the High Court of Justice and can be exercised by any judge of the High Court."*

Further, in R. v Central Independent Television Plc[2] Waite LJ said:

> *'the prerogative jurisdiction has shown striking versatility throughout its long history in adapting its powers to the protective needs of children, encompassing all kinds of different situations. Although the jurisdiction is theoretically boundless, the courts have, nevertheless, found it necessary to set self imposed limits upon its exercise, for the sake of clarity and consistency and of avoiding conflict between child welfare and other public advantages'.*

To consider it in a fairly modern context, Ward LJ in *Re* Z (A Minor) (Identification: Restrictions on Publication)[3] Ward LJ said:

> *'The wardship or inherent jurisdiction of the court to cast its cloak of protection over minors whose interests are at risk of harm is unlimited in theory though in practice the judges who exercise the jurisdiction have created classes of cases in which the court will not exercise its powers'*

In 2018, the then President of the Family Division, Sir James Munby, published official guidance on the jurisdiction of the family court titled: 'ALLOCATION OF CASES WITHIN THE FAMILY COURT TO

---

2 [1994] Fam 192, paragraphs 207 – 208

3 [1997] Fam 1, para 23

HIGH COURT JUDGE LEVEL AND TRANSFER OF CASES FROM THE FAMILY COURT TO THE HIGH COURT'[4].

In the guidance, Sir James Munby set out the relationship between the family court and the High Court. He went on to state at paragraph 4:

> *"The High Court, of which the Family Division is part, is a superior court of record. It has unlimited jurisdiction. The family court, in contrast, is a creature of statute, with its jurisdiction defined by statute. The jurisdiction of the family court, although very extensive, is not unlimited"*

The key phrase in the guidance is that in respect of the '*unlimited jurisdiction*'. The guidance goes on to give various examples of cases, which must commence in the High Court. In the first part of the schedule at Part A, it states that '*family court does not have jurisdiction; must be commenced in the Family Division*'. They are:

> *'1 Inherent jurisdiction of the court relating to children (including applications for interim relief and injunctions invoking the inherent jurisdiction of the court and applications to make a child a ward of court or to bring such an order to an end)'*

The above is useful in illustrating the power of the inherent jurisdiction. In contrast to most of the family law proceedings which are heard in the Family Court, the High Court is in a unique position in that it can exercise and invoke the inherent jurisdiction.

Wardship

An interesting feature of High Court proceedings is the difference between the inherent jurisdiction and wardship. Both areas are dealt with in the High Court, but whilst they are at times linked, they must be

4 https://www.judiciary.uk/wp-content/uploads/2018/02/pfd-guidance-2018-jurisdiction.pdf

separated as otherwise practitioners fall into a trap of seeking certain relief that is not necessary. It is a common misconception that the subject children have to be made wards in order for the court to exercise its inherent jurisdiction. This is not the case. The Family Procedure Rules ['FPR'] helpfully distil this myth and they distinguish the different characteristics of wardship. For example, the FPR 2010[5] defines[6] the distinguishing characteristics of wardship as follows:

> "*(a) custody of a child who is a ward is vested in the court; and*
>
> *(b) although day to day care and control of the ward is given to an individual or to a local authority, no important step can be taken in the child's life without the court's consent*"

In terms of a case law example, Parker J in AB v CD[7] stated the following:

> '*Wardship is a way in which the 'inherent jurisdiction with regard to children' (ie the parens patriae jurisdiction) may be exercised. Once a child is a ward of court, that child is under the continuous protection of the court, even after a final order has been made determining the issues in respect of that child. Once a child is ward of court that child's place or country of residence or school cannot be changed without a court order*'.

5 Practice Direction 12D, para 1.3

6 Ibid, para 1.3 (a) and (b)

7 [2014] 1 FLR 1439, para 51

What does the inherent jurisdiction consider?

It is important to note that the inherent jurisdiction is concerned with the welfare of the subject children. In the Matter of NY (A Child)[8] at paragraph 49, Lord Wilson commended the use of the welfare checklist in the context of the inherent jurisdiction:

> *'...their utility in any analysis of a child welfare has been recognised for nearly 30 years. In its determination of an application under the inherent jurisdiction governed by consideration of a child's welfare, the court is likely to find it appropriate to consider the first six aspects of welfare specified in section 1(3)... and, if it is considering whether to make a summary order, it will initially examine whether, in order to sufficiently to identify what the child's welfare requires, it should conduct an inquiry and, if so, how extensive that enquiry should be'.*

Therefore, when a party is seeking to advance a case pursuant to the inherent jurisdiction, the court will have in mind the welfare checklist specified in Section 1(3) Children Act 1989. These provisions within the Children Act will be considered in respect of every decision that is made pursuant to the inherent jurisdiction.

Proceedings in the High Court

This book will make it clear in later chapters why proceedings relating to the inherent jurisdiction is in the High Court. Practitioners should be aware of the allocation guidance. Whether the proceedings are private or public law in nature, there are other reasons why proceedings may be allocated to a judge of a High Court level. It does not necessarily mean that the inherent jurisdiction is automatically being engaged or exercised. It might be due to the level of complexity of a case that a High Court judge is required, and this should always be differentiated from what the inherent jurisdiction entails.

---

8 [2019] UKSC 49

Conclusion

As this chapter outlines, the inherent jurisdiction by its origins has a deep-rooted history. Its purpose is clear, which is to assist in the protection of children. How this can be achieved will be considered throughout this book. As this chapter outlines, there are numerous case law examples and powerful quotes as to the purpose of the inherent jurisdiction. However, what practitioners must note is firstly, it is the High Court that exercises the inherent jurisdiction and as outlined in the allocation guidance, proceedings must be before a High Court judge (or deputy) to enable the inherent jurisdiction to be exercised and considered. Secondly, practitioners must not get confused between the concepts of wardship and inherent jurisdiction. The inherent jurisdiction can be utilised to secure wide-ranging powers and children do not necessarily need to be made wards of the High Court, albeit there are circumstances where this may exist. Nonetheless, when it does exist, the central power being utilised remains the inherent jurisdiction. Further, this book will however outline through case law examples that there may be exceptional circumstances where a child could be made a ward of the court and the inherent jurisdiction is being utilised also, but the powers being used can be separated.

CHAPTER TWO

PROCEDURE TO COMMENCE PROCEEDINGS

Introduction

In this chapter, the procedure for commencing applications under the inherent jurisdiction will be considered. It is important practitioners are alert to the rules and guidance provided to ensure the matter can be heard effectively.

Commencing Inherent Jurisdiction proceedings

As will be outlined in this book, a number of different parties can commence proceedings in the High Court under the inherent jurisdiction. However, at the outset, there are two ways this can be achieved. A new non-existent application can be made in the High Court or secondly, existing proceedings can be reallocated to High Court level to enable the inherent jurisdiction to be considered.

The Application

The application form to issue is the C66[9]. This is the application form in respect of invoking the inherent jurisdiction. In practice, the C66 form is accompanied by a separate C1A form. The purpose of this form is to provide supplementary information when making allegations of harm and domestic abuse.

---

9 Practitioners must note it is not the C67 form. The C67 form is utilised for child abduction cases for example the 1980 Hague Convention

The C1A can have an important evidential basis. The form is the first opportunity for an applicant to set out in a table form the allegations that they wish to raise. More importantly, Section 3 of the C1A form includes a heading titled '*abduction*' and asks for information about any possible abduction/threats of abduction as well as information about passports the children may have. Section 5 of the C1A specifically asks the applicant to set out what steps are sought to protect the applicant and/or the children. Therefore, an applicant such as a parent or the state through the Local Authority can make an application.

Applications such as the C66 and C1A must be signed off by a statement of truth from either the applicant (if acting in person) or the solicitor representing the applicant. The forms therefore have evidential status in the proceedings and may be referred to throughout the course of the proceeding. However, whilst the forms ask relevant questions to enable the court to ascertain the urgency of the situation, the orders sought and why the inherent jurisdiction should be utilised, ultimately it has to be acknowledged that the forms are quite brief in nature. Consequently, in practice, the applications are often accompanied by a witness statement and the Family Procedure Rules set out this requirement[10]. This witness statement can be directly from the applicant or if this is not possible, from the solicitor with conduct of the case. This statement will set out the factual basis, highlight the key issues and explain why certain orders are sought by the applicant.

Re-allocation

The alternative to proceedings commencing in the High Court at the outset is that proceedings can be commenced in the local Family Court first. Following on from this, there might be a specific issue or a reason why proceedings require a High Court judge or any other reason why the inherent jurisdiction may be utilised. For example, in the middle of private law disputes between parents, a complicated issue could arise

10 FPR 2010, PD12J para 3.4

relating to vaccinations or abduction and as such, the proceedings need to be reallocated to the High Court. Alternatively, within public law proceedings the local authority may have a public law order such as an interim care order, vesting in them parental responsibility, but then a significant issue arises in respect of medical treatment or abduction which requires orders through the inherent jurisdiction. In these circumstances, directions can be sought from any level of judge for proceedings to be reallocated to High Court level. If this reallocation does form part of a court order, the order should specifically set out the reason why. Each local court has a Designated Family Judge who would be a Circuit Judge. In many circumstances, a request from this Designated Family Judge to the High Court judge can be made to explore the case if there are any issue as to the appropriateness of reallocation.

Types of Hearings

Ex Parte Hearings

As the inherent jurisdiction has wide-ranging powers, the powers are often sought to be utilised in the most urgent situations. For example, if there is a sudden risk of child abduction or a child has already been abducted. Or, if there is some other form of risk resulting in a party having no choice but to apply ex-parte. Ex-parte hearings are also known as without notice hearings. There is a tremendous amount of case law of the need to properly consider whether a hearing should be ex-parte or not, because it is one-sided in nature and therefore the other side can be seriously disadvantaged.

In the High Court, ex-parte hearings are heard before the allocated urgent applications judge. Each day, there is an allocated urgent applications judge who sits in-person in the Royal Courts of Justice, Strand, London, or remotely given the court's jurisdiction is for the whole of England and Wales. In practice, applications can be issued in advance with the Listings Office with a request that it should be made before the urgent applications judge, or they can be issued on the day depending on the level of urgency in existence.

The Process – Ex-parte hearing

In the High Court context, the court is concerned with the welfare of the subject children. There may be various reasons for why a hearing is ex-parte and there may be many ex-parte hearings before notice of the proceedings, or the orders are given to the respondent. The degree to which this can happen varies.

In terms of guidance, the starting point for practitioners is the FPR 2010, R12.47 which sets out what applications can be considered on an ex-parte basis. There is a long list, but the relevant ones for cases relating to the inherent jurisdiction are:

- for the disclosure of relevant information as to where the child is; and
- or a collection order, location order or passport order ['tipstaff orders'];

In 2018, the previous President of the Family Division, Sir James Mundy, released guidance on the 'Case Management and Mediation of International Child Abduction Proceedings'[11]. This document is useful guidance for all practitioners that have a case in the High Court.

The guidance is particularly helpful as it is tailored towards the typical cases in the High Court. At paragraph 2.1, it emphasises:

> *'Commencing proceedings by way of a without notice application pursuant to FPR r 12.47 will be justified only where (a) the case is one of exceptional urgency or (b) there is a compelling case that the child's welfare will be compromised if the other party is alerted in advance or*

[11] https://www.judiciary.uk/wp-content/uploads/2018/03/presidents-practice-guidance-case-management-mediation-of-international-child-abduction-proceedings-20180227.pdf

> *(c) where the whereabouts of the child and the proposed respondent are unknown'*

In the guidance, it is further emphasised that evidence in support of an ex-parte hearing '*must be as detailed and precise as possible*'[12]. The guidance places key markers on practitioners to set out the proposed risks and why the hearing must be conducted without notice and for what purpose (for example, what orders are sought and why).

The evidence in support of a without notice application must be as detailed and precise as possible to enable the court to have the full information available. Practitioners should consider the appropriateness of without notice hearings and have regard to the comments of Mostyn J in ES v LS[13]. At paragraph 27 – 29, his lordship commented the following about procedural unfairness and the frequency in which without notice orders are made:

> '*Ex parte orders are intrinsically unfair. They are unfair because the court hears only from one side. They can only be justified where there is a well-founded belief that the giving of notice would lead to irretrievable prejudice being caused to the applicant or where there is some exceptional urgency so that there is literally no time to give notice: ND v KP (Freezing Order: Ex Parte Application) [2011] EWHC 457 (Fam) at paras 10–12, CEF Holdings Ltd & Anor v City Electrical Factors Ltd & Ors [2012] EWHC 1524 (QB) at para 235; R v R (Family Court: Procedural Fairness) [2014] EWFC 48 at para 1; Practice Guidance (Family Courts: Without Notice Orders) [2017] 1 WLR 478.*
>
> *The case law has emphasised the adverse consequences for litigants and their advisers if the requirements are not observed and applications are made which are wanting in candour or otherwise improper. It is*

---

12 Ibid, para 2.2

13 [2021] EWHC 2758

noteworthy that in the Administrative Court, where there has been for years gross abuse of the Immediates facility, sanctions are now meted out to delinquent practitioners who have sought to gain an illegitimate litigation advantage by making spurious urgent one-sided applications to the Immediates judge: see R (DVP) v SSHD [2021] EWHC 603 (Admin); Re the Court's exercise of the Hamid jurisdiction [2021] EWHC 1895 (Admin). The most usual sanction is a summons to attend a public sitting of what is known as the Hamid court in order to be openly, and shamingly, admonished.

Historically, in the field of child abduction it was considered acceptable, almost normal, to start virtually every case off with an ex parte location order. Old habits die hard and this one has been particularly sturdy, surviving not merely the robust decision of Sir James Munby P in the Court of Appeal in A v A, but his equally tough Guidance of 13 March 2018, set out above. The time has surely come to insist that the standards in the Practice Guidance concerning ex parte applications are scrupulously observed'

In 2023, the President of the Family Division released guidance titled: 'Presidents Guidance: Case Management and Mediation of International Child Abduction Proceedings'[14]. Paragraph 1 (b) of the guidance relates specifically to inherent jurisdiction proceedings in the context of child abduction cases. It states the guidance relates to matters concerning:

'The High Court's power to make an order returning the child to another jurisdiction or to make an order for the return of the child to this jurisdiction ("the inherent jurisdiction")'

14 https://www.judiciary.uk/wp-content/uploads/2023/03/Presidents-Practice-Guidance-on-Case-Management-and-Mediation-of-International-Child-Abduction-Proceedings.pdf

This guidance does consider some important principles relating to ex-parte hearings and the use of the inherent jurisdiction. The President acknowledges at paragraph 2.6:

> *'It is recognised that many applications relating to alleged child abduction will meet the criteria for without notice applications'.*

The President goes on to state the current requirements for ex-parte hearings as follows:

'2.2. The evidence in support of a without notice application must be as detailed and precise as possible, having regard both to the material provided by the applicant and transmitted by the Central Authority of the Requesting State and the high duty of candor required with respect to without notice applications. Unparticularised generalities will not suffice. Sources of hearsay must be identified, and expressions of opinion must be supported by evidence and proper reasoning. The evidence should set out the orders sought, together with fully particularised reasons. Specifically, with respect to the narrow circumstances justifying a without notice application set out in para 2.1 above:

> *(a) Where the justification for proceeding without notice is said to be exceptional urgency, the evidence in support of the without notice application must identify why the case is exceptionally urgent and why no notice, even short informal notice, can be given to the respondent (with respect to short, informal notice see para 2.7 below).*
>
> *(b) Where the justification for proceeding without notice is said to be a compelling case that the child's welfare will be compromised if notice is given, the evidence in support of the without notice application must demonstrate a real risk that, if the respondent is alerted in advance, the welfare of the child will be compromised, whether by the respondent thwarting the court's order or otherwise. Where the risk is said to be the removal of the child from the jurisdiction, the evidence must address (i) the magnitude of the risk that the respondent will be minded to remove, (ii) the magnitude of the risk that, if the respondent is*

minded to remove, he or she will be able to evade protective measures put in place by the court and (iii) the magnitude of the consequences for the child if the protective measures are evaded.

(c) Where the justification for proceeding without notice is said to be that the whereabouts of the child and the proposed respondent are unknown, the evidence in support of the without notice application must explain what steps have been taken to locate them, what disclosure orders are required against an identified agency and why there is reason to believe that that agency may be able to provide information which may lead to the location of the child'.

The above is drafted in very clear terms and with particular acknowledgment of the urgency that can arise in inherent jurisdiction cases relating to child abduction. Practitioners must have regard to the guidance when preparing for ex-parte hearings and also when specifying the reasons why the matter is pursued ex-parte.

The chapters concerning child abduction and the inherent jurisdiction will consider some of the orders that can be made ex-parte through the inherent jurisdiction.

Multiple Parties

In some proceedings there can be multiple parties. For example, in public law proceedings there could be a respondent mother, respondent father and the respondent children (through their guardian). Accordingly, a Local Authority in these circumstances have to consider whether to give notice to any other party. For example, the respondent parents may be a cause of risk or have unlawfully abducted a child and therefore proceedings may be on notice to the guardian on behalf of the subject children only. The Court order should record who the hearing was without notice to and why.

Tipstaff Orders

One matter that is unique to inherent jurisdiction proceedings in the ability to obtain Tipstaff orders. There are many different reasons for why a Tipstaff order may be sought. Typically, these are only sought by applicant to proceedings, the local authority in public law proceedings or proceedings relating to the protection of children, such as when a local authority is seeking a Forced Marriage Protection Order or Female Genital Mutilation Order.

Before considering applying for a Tipstaff orders, practitioners must contact Tipstaff before seeking any order from the High Court relating to Tipstaff orders. The Tipstaff possess the ultimate experience in all matters relating to abduction and other risks associated with matters in the High Court. Their advice is necessary and they have their own forms to complete and often the judge will check with Tipstaff as to their views on the orders sought.

If any Tipstaff orders are made at court, they will be drafted by the Court Associate and not the practitioner. The precedent orders are available to enable practitioners to consider the terms and implications of such orders, however they are always drafted by the associate.

As a point of first reference, practitioners should consider the FPR, PD12D, Rule 7.1 – 7.4. These rules briefly set out the role of Tipstaff:

> '*7.1*
>
> *The tipstaff is the enforcement officer for all orders made in the High Court. The tipstaff's jurisdiction extends throughout England and Wales. Every applicable order made in the High Court is addressed to the tipstaff in children and family matters (eg 'The Court hereby directs the Tipstaff of the High Court of Justice, whether acting by himself or his assistants or a police officer as follows…').*

7.2

The tipstaff may effect an arrest and then inform the police. Sometimes the local bailiff or police will detain a person in custody until the tipstaff arrives to collect that person or give further directions as to the disposal of the matter. The tipstaff may also make a forced entry although there will generally be a uniformed police officer standing by to make sure there is no breach of the peace.

7.3

There is only one tipstaff (with two assistants) but the tipstaff can also call on any constable or bailiff to assist in carrying out the tipstaff's duties.

7.4

The majority of the tipstaff's work involves locating children and taking them into protective custody, including cases of child abduction abroad'

<u>*Passport Orders*</u>

If the applicant has set out in the witness statement that there is a risk the respondent may seek to evade participating in any court proceedings or may be a flight risk to another country, then a passport order may be necessary. A passport order includes various prohibitions with a penal notice attached to it (in the event the respondent breaches any order, an application for committal can be made). A passport order is addressed to the respondent who must hand over any travel document (such as a passport, ID cards) to the Tipstaff and the respondent will be prohibited from seeking to obtain or apply for further travel documents. Equally, the passport order will include prohibitions to ensure that the respondent and children must not leave the jurisdiction and a port alert is created. The port alert will flag up any attempt of a person leaving the jurisdiction or entering the jurisdiction. If any third party stands in the way of compliance with a passport order, then the police also have powers over them as well. For example, if Tipstaff seek to execute a passport order at a property but a non-subject party is evasive and making it difficult for Tipstaff to execute the order, then they themselves can get into trouble.

Mr Justice Cobb in Re P (Discharge of Passport Order)[15] provided useful guidance in respect of passport orders. Practitioners on both sides of the coin, those seeking a passport order or those seeking a discharge of passport order should refer to this authority. His lordship stated after reviewing the relevant authorities:

> *'Tipstaff passport order is a useful tool in the judicial armoury, particularly in circumstances where:*
>
> *(i) a court needs to take urgent action to try to prevent a parent from removing a child out of the country (see Wilson J as he then was in B v B (Injunction: Restraint on Leaving Jurisdiction) [1997] 2 FLR 148 remarked at p.153: 'B v B [1997]');*
>
> *(ii) where there is an assessed risk that a foreign parent may misuse a period of contact in England in order to remove a child overseas (again, B v B [1997] at p.153);*
>
> *(iii) where (as here) the court wishes to ensure the attendance of a person at a court hearing within the jurisdiction, and there is a risk that, absent such an order, the person may flee the country before doing so (see for instance Thorpe J as he then was in Re S (Financial Provision: Non-Resident) [1996] 1 FCR 148); and (iv) where without such an order the execution of an interlocutory order may be stymied (B v B [1997] at p.154).*

15 [2020] EWHC 3009 (Fam), at paragraphs 31 – 40

> *32. But a passport order is a potent order, with significant implications, whose use it seems to me should be tightly controlled; thus:*
>
> *i) A passport order should only ever be made for a finite period of time (this is likely to be, as it was in this case, for a period of six months before it would have expired unexecuted) (see Re L (A Child), Re Oddin [2016] EWCA Civ 173);*
>
> *ii) A passport order should not be made where the sole purpose is to coerce the respondent into action of a particular kind; in his submissions, the father rightly referenced in this regard Hobhouse LJ's judgment in B v B [1994] 2 FLR 479 at 486 and Sir James Munby P in Re B (A Child: Evidence: Passport Order) [2014] EWCA Civ 843, [2015] 1 FCR 75, [2015] 1 FLR 871 at [33]'*

Practitioners must ensure that they have the exact spelling of the respondent's name and the children's names to ensure the port alerts can be registered as appropriate and the children/respondent do not leave the jurisdiction. Practitioners must ensure that they take instructions from the applicant in respect of all possible travel documents/passports the respondent and children may have. This is because when the passport order is executed, the relevant documents can be sought and seized. At court, the barrister or solicitor must complete the tipstaff forms and include all relevant information. Upon the order being made by the judge, the Court Associate will have regard to the forms and compile the tipstaff order. If there is a spelling mistake in the names or dates of birth, then the port alert might not be flagged up and triggered. Therefore, in cases where abduction is sought to be prevented, if there is a spelling mistake in existence, abduction might happen. It is crucial that practitioners check all Tipstaff orders for errors before they are executed.

A port alert is a useful tool that is contained within Tipstaff orders such as a passport order. If a party is seeking a port alert, then as Mostyn J indicated in A v B (Port Alert)[16] at paragraph 42 outlined: '*the initial application for a port alert order will almost invariably be made ex parte for obvious reasons*'. Practitioners should however note in the decision of A v B, Mostyn J did highlight the procedure for port alerts to be made in the local family court as opposed to the High Court. There are differences to the procedure and purpose. Mostyn J outlined the following process and reasoning as paragraphs 37 to 40 of his judgment:

> '*In my judgment, therefore, the Family Court plainly does have the power to issue a freestanding port alert order, where such an order is justified on the facts and is an incidental and supplemental order to give effect to a decision of the Family Court.*
>
> *The most obvious example is the situation where the Family Court has made a prohibited steps order preventing parents from taking a child out of the country without the other's consent or a court order. A port alert in such circumstances is simply acting as a supplemental safety net to ensure the efficacy of the prohibited steps order. It would be highly anomalous if the Family Court had power to issue a bench warrant to bring a parent who had gone on the run with the children before the court but did not have the power to issue a port alert order to prevent the children leaving the country.*
>
> *I would not expect freestanding port alert orders to be made by the Family Court routinely. Such an order should only be made where the applicant demonstrates with clear evidence that there is a real and imminent risk that the children in question will be removed from England and Wales. When assessing that risk the court will not demand proof that it is more likely than not that the children will be removed; it will, nonetheless, still expect proof of a degree of probability not far short of that standard. It is important that applications for these*

16 [2021] EWHC 1716 (Fam)

> *orders are not made in reliance on evidence which amounts to no more than mere assertion or which is otherwise flimsy or unsubstantiated.*
>
> *When such an order is made the default position should be that it lasts for only 28 days in the first instance and that any extension of that period should only be ordered on a subsequent inter partes hearing. In my opinion this is a key provision which needs to be adhered to strictly'*

Therefore, there is a difference relating to a prohibited steps order and a port alert. For the purposes of this book, what practitioners need to know is that if proceedings are in the High Court and the inherent jurisdiction is being utilised, Tipstaff will be responsible (if a order is made) for enacting a port alert which are contained within their orders. Notwithstanding this, practitioners must be on high alert. Given there is the power for the Family Court to make a freestanding port alert, practitioners can be expected to explain as to why a Tipstaff order is preferred and necessary. There may be a number of reasons for this For example, it could be submitted that the proceedings will need to remain in the High Court in any event for a number of complex reasons or due to the fact that a port alert by Tipstaff is enacted fairly fast, often on the same day and further, Tipstaff orders enables Tipstaff to do an international movement trace to ascertain whether the respondent and children have left England and Wales, and if so when and how which might be important evidence relating to the case or strategy to be adopted

Location Order

A location order is often sought at the first hearing with disclosure orders. The purpose of a location order is to locate the relevant children and respondent. It includes all the similar provisions that appear in the passport order in respect of the prohibitions and port alert. However, a location order once served on someone must inform the Tipstaff of the whereabouts of the subject children or any known information to assist the Tipstaff in locating the children. A location order often works in tandem with a disclosure order. For example, once a disclosure order reveals the last known address of the respondent then this information is provided by the solicitor for the applicant to Tipstaff who will then seek to execute the order.

Collection Orders

A collection order will contain all the provisions of a passport order, in the sense that a port alert will be enacted, and the passports of the respondents will be seised and held by Tipstaff if found. However, a collection order has a very specific purpose. It is an order requiring Tipstaff to collect and return a child or place the child with someone else. For example, in public law proceedings a Local Authority may not be able to find a subject child or a child in their care may have vanished and is with a parent or someone else. A collection order will enable the subject child to be placed back to the care and control of the Local Authority. Or alternatively, in private law proceedings there may be a Child Arrangements Order for a child to live with a specific parent. The other parent may not be happy with this outcome or may breach this order. In these circumstances, a collection order can be sought to ensure the child is returned to the named individual, such as a parent.

One point to emphasise about a collection order is that it is a Tipstaff order. In the private law context, practitioners should consider whether a recovery order is more suitable. This equally applies to a Local Authority in public law proceedings. A recovery order can be made by a family law judge in the context of public or private law proceedings. The order will specify that a named police force are to recover the child and place the child in the applicant's care (such as a parent in private law proceedings, or a local authority in public law proceedings). In contrast, within inherent jurisdiction High Court proceedings, a collection order may be particularly attractive in circumstances where it is believed that there may be real risk to the subject child, by means of harm, abduction or if the child has become difficult to locate by means of absconding a placement.

Tipstaff Orders being executed

A Tipstaff order being executed has two forms of impact. Firstly, the respondent will be alerted to the fact there are now court proceedings in existence (albeit Tipstaff will not serve the court documentation on them) and has their own and the children's travel documents seised and informed about the other prohibitions as contained within the Tipstaff order. Upon this happening, the solicitors for the applicant must arrange for personal service of the documents to be served on the respondent so that they are aware of what has happened and to be informed about the next court date. Secondly, the respondent no longer has the travel documents of their own or the children's travel documents in their possession. These are instead held by Tipstaff either until the conclusion of the court proceedings or further order of the court. The issue in respect of Tipstaff orders must be considered at each and every hearing, and Tipstaff will provide the standard wording that needs to be included in the order in the event that an existing Tipstaff order is extended, varied or discharged.

Continuation of Tipstaff Orders

As the Presidents guidance in 2018 acknowledged:

> '*Passport orders, location orders and collection orders constitute an interference with the child's and the respondent's fundamental rights. On a without notice application, parties should only seek, and the court can only be expected to grant, such orders as are necessary and proportionate having regard to the risks assessed to exist on the evidence*'[17]

Once an order has been made, it is likely the order will continue until they are executed. For example, if the respondent and children cannot be

17 https://www.judiciary.uk/wp-content/uploads/2018/03/presidents-practice-guidance-case-management-mediation-of-international-child-abduction-proceedings-20180227.pdf para 2.4

found then the order will be extended at each without notice hearing. In terms of the law about continuation of Tipstaff orders, practitioners should note the comments of the Court of Appeal in *Re K (Forced Marriage: Passport Order)*[18]

> *'… an open-ended passport order or travel ban should only be imposed in the most exceptional of cases and where the court can look sufficiently far into the future to be satisfied that highly restrictive orders of that nature will be required indefinitely. In all other cases, the court should impose a time limit when making such orders. The time limit will vary from case-to-case and, like all other elements, be a bespoke provision imposing a restriction only in so far as that is justified on the facts as found. Unless the court can see with clarity that there will be no need for any continuing order after a particular date, for example when it is clear that the circumstances will change so that the risk is removed, the appropriate course will be for the court to list the matter for further review a short time before the passport and/or travel ban will otherwise expire'*

And[19]:

> *'A travel ban and a Passport Order are highly intrusive in terms of their impact upon the private life and freedom of movement of the individual concerned'*

Cobb J in Re P[20] further stated:

> *'Furthermore, once granted and passports are seized:-*
>
> *iii) The passport order is unlikely to endure beyond the conclusion of the proceedings in which the order is made (Re M (Children) (Care*

18 [2020] EWCA Civ 19, at para 67

19 Ibid, at para 77

20 [2020] EWHC 3009 (Fam), at para 32

Proceedings: Passport Orders) [2017] EWCA Civ 69*). If an order for a passport to be held indefinitely can ever be justified (i.e. after the conclusion of proceedings), it is likely only to be in an unusual and probably quite extreme case where it can be demonstrated, after a close evaluation of the degree of risk to the children and of the harm to which they will be exposed if the risk becomes a reality, that such a serious invasion of the passport-holder's rights is proportionate and necessary: Re M (above); cf, Re A (A Child)* [2016] EWCA Civ 572, *[2016] 4 WLR 111, paras 69-70;*

iv) Consistent with the principles above, and the observations from the authorities, it seems to me to be incumbent on the court to keep under careful review during ongoing proceedings the need to deprive a person of their passport, under a tipstaff passport order; such an order should not remain in place for any longer than is necessary to achieve the legitimate desired protection or outcome.

The removal of an individual's passport, even on a temporary basis, be that of an adult or child, is a very significant incursion into the individual's freedom and personal autonomy. It is never an order that can be made lightly (Hayden J in London Borough of Tower Hamlets v M [2015] EWHC 869); a passport order should in my judgment rarely if ever be more than a very temporary measure'

On-Notice hearings

The alternative to ex-parte hearings are on-notice hearings. This would enable the respondent to have sufficient time to instruct lawyers and be represented, if possible, at the first hearing.

Conclusion

It is apparent from the contents of this chapter that there are key considerations practitioners must keep in mind in cases when proceedings utilising the inherent jurisdiction is being pursued. Through the inherent jurisdiction, there are a number of strategies that can be adopted to locate the respondent and children, but the evidence must justify such orders. Further, to seek a continuation of the orders requires justification and proportionality. Once proceedings are on-notice then it is important evidence is timetabled and the issue of a fact-finding hearing is considered at the earliest possible stage if it is necessary. The question for practitioners at the stage of on-notice hearings is to assess what the trajectory of the case is and what issues the court is going to need to determine. Once this is ascertained, proceedings can be duly timetabled.

CHAPTER THREE

ORDERS MADE UNDER THE INHERENT JURISDICTION

Introduction

This chapter will consider some generic orders that can be made in the context of inherent jurisdiction. A number of these orders can be made in the context of public, private or international family law proceedings. In later chapters, the types of orders and the purpose of such orders in specific areas of the law will be considers. In contrast, this chapter will look at some of the overarching orders.

Ex-parte orders

As chapter 2 outlined, there are a number of rules for ex-parte hearings. In proceedings relating to the inherent jurisdiction, many cases commence by virtue of ex-parte hearings.

One of the biggest reasons why proceedings may need to commence ex-parte is because the applicant may not know the whereabouts of the respondent and children. The first step is to locate the respondent and the subject children. There may be means by which the application could be on notice, for example, the respondent's mobile or email address may be known. Notwithstanding this, the question is that of risk. If it turns out to be true that there is a real risk to the child by virtue of harm or abduction for example, then alerting the respondent / giving notice that an application is going to be made to locate the respondent and children may defeat the ultimate purpose; to locate them. Tipping the respondent off without appropriate safeguarding can cause the respondent to flee the jurisdiction or make it even more difficult to locate them. Therefore, it is necessary to obtain appropriate safeguards to locate the respondent and children before this risk alleged materialises which will be considered in this chapter.

Disclosure Orders to Locate

A party by seek the use of the inherent jurisdiction to locate a respondent or children, whether they are subject to proceedings or not. Disclosure orders are a powerful tool within inherent jurisdiction proceedings but before they can be obtained certain procedures have to be compiled with to enable them to be granted and to also make them effective.

The starting point is the Family Procedure Rules. Rule 21.2 covers '*orders for disclosure against a person who is not a party*' and such orders can be made utilising the inherent jurisdiction. A disclosure order is an order made by the High Court on a non-party directing them to disclose to the court or the applicant's solicitors any information the non-party has in relation to the whereabouts of the children and respondent. The non-party can be a person, such as a family member of the respondent, or a government body[21], such as the Department of Work and Pensions, the NHS, Department of Education, HM Passport Office or any business / organisation such as a bank, a phone company and other business entity. Practitioners should keep an eye on any government body changing their name which often happens, because the disclosure order will need to be addressed to the right government body / department. In addition to naming the organisation or government body, words including in the order should also address the 'responsible person or agent acting on behalf of [the organisation]'.

There is no hard rule, but the court will always have in mind the need to be proportionate when it comes to deciding which disclosure orders to obtain. If the court is satisfied on the evidence from the C66 form and witness statement that there are grounds to obtain a disclosure order, then there is often a proportionate limit of three or four. In order to save costs

21 See FPR 2010, PD12F, para 4.18

and court time, practitioners need to think carefully about what type of disclosure orders should be sought. For example, if it is known the children are of school age then the Department of Education may be appropriate to ascertain if there's any address associated with a school place. Further, if it thought that the respondent may be claiming state benefits then the Department of Work and Pensions maybe useful. Other options can consist of disclosure orders against other department bodies and the NHS.

Practitioners must be very careful about suggesting disclosure orders against family members. Again, the question is that of risk. Is there a risk the family member will contact the respondent and ask what is going on? If so, then the respondent will be tipped off.

There are a number of precedents readily available on the internet for disclosure orders which are regularly updated. Practitioners need to be aware and ensure the draft orders contain the relevant information:

- The organisation / government body / individual has the right to apply to the High Court to vary / discharge the disclosure order on notice;

- The order must include provisions for costs. For example, if the organisation may spend money in looking through records to locate the address, such costings can be reimbursed. If the applicant has a legal aid certificate then practitioners must ensure that any costs associated with the disclosure order is deemed a reasonable and proportionate disbursement on the legal aid certificate of the relevant party;

- As a result of the issue of risk, the order can include a provision (sometimes set out in bold) that the person / organisation who is subject to the disclosure order must not inform the respondent of the making of the order;

- As disclosure orders are often made ex-parte, practitioners should record on the face of the order as recital the reason why the order was made without notice;

- There is an expectation that the solicitor for the applicant will offer an undertaking to only use the address provided by the disclosure orders for the purposes of informing tipstaff to execute their order / service of the documents. This is important because at this initial stage of proceedings, no findings of fact can be made and because it is an ex-parte hearing the court only has the benefit of hearing one sides version of events. Therefore, to be safe and to ameliorate any risk this undertaking is expected. In the alternative, the court can through the inherent jurisdiction order that the address must not be disclosed to the applicant until further order of the court;

- The jurisdictional basis of the disclosure order should be specified in the order, which is that the order was made pursuant to the inherent jurisdiction. The purpose of the disclosure order may also be necessary; and

- The order needs to specify how long the organisation / person has to provide the information to the applicant. It is important to be realistic. In reality, if an order is made by the High Court then it is probably because there is an element of urgency but requiring the organisation to provide disclosure in 7-days maybe unrealistic. The business / organisation may be very large and there may be a backlog.

Government bodies often have their own systems for processing disclosure orders, likewise, do some major organisations such as banks and such information are usually available on the internet. It is important practitioners chase the sealed order from the court in order to avoid delay. There is no point serving an approved order which appears in draft form, for the organisation to take several weeks to look at it to respond stating they need a sealed order. Further, solicitors responsible for serving the orders should undertake research beforehand to ascertain how the organisation will process the disclosure order. For example, some organisations / government bodies have a particular email address where the sealed order must be sent to or their own portal online.

Disclosure Order to gather information

Disclosure orders to locate the subject children or respondent may not always be successful. Alternatively, throughout the course of proceedings it may be necessary to gather further information about the respondent on an ex-parte basis. Through the inherent jurisdiction, disclosure orders need not only focus on the locating / last known address of a respondent / the children. Disclosure orders are far-reaching. For example, if the respondent's address is not known but the applicant may recall that they have seen the respondent use a bank account with a known bank account, then a disclosure order can be made against that bank. The disclosure order can be asked to reveal all the bank account details associated with the respondent's name together with perhaps recent bank statements. This information once provided will enable the legal representatives or the court to inspect the disclosure to ascertain whether there are any clues to locate the respondent. Likewise, disclosure orders can be obtained against mobile phone companies. Such disclosure can reveal times and locations in which calls can be made. These orders are more invasive as it will reveal very sensitive and personal information and again, proportionality is key and the necessity of such an order.

Attendance Orders

In cases in the High Court where the inherent jurisdiction is invoked another option is to secure the attendance at court of non-parties for the purposes of obtaining further information. These types of orders, referred to as 'attendance orders' are common in cases in the inherent jurisdiction and generally in proceedings relating to child abduction where the necessity of such an order is satisfied.

In circumstances where disclosure orders are not successful and the location of the respondent and / or the children remain unknown then the next step is to consider what else can be utilised to locate them. As outlined above, disclosure orders can be wide-ranging on government bodies but also on phone networks and banks. In the scenario when these disclosure orders are not successful then an attendance, order should be considered. Practitioners should find out from their client, the stranded parent whether the respondent has any family members / friends in England and Wales who are likely to know their whereabouts. If so, an application can be made for their attendance at court together with a witness statement outlining any information they have in their knowledge. The order must be accompanied by the standard wording, in that the family member has the liberty to apply to the court to vary / discharge the order and they should take legal advice. Further, if practitioners download and access the draft precedents of the orders it will be apparent there is a notice that has to appear on the face of the order warning the individual that an application can be made for a bench warrant in the event the individual fails to comply with the order. This will provide for Tipstaff to arrest the individual and bring them to court.

If the applicant does not know the address of the family / friends, then disclosure orders can also be sought against these non-parties utilising the inherent jurisdiction.

If the person to who is subject to an attendance order fails to comply and does not attend court, then an application can be made on behalf of the party for a bench warrant. This will involve Tipstaff attending the property to bring the individual to court. Once at court, the individual can be cross-examined and asked questions to ascertain the whereabouts of the respondent and / or children. Practitioners should obtain a transcript of the evidence in case any future application is made relating to contempt if it can be proven the individual lied during evidence on oath.

Conclusion

This chapter outlines that when the issue of risk arises, there are a number of orders that can be made under the inherent jurisdiction. These orders have to be made for a specific purpose. As later chapters will consider, there are a number of other considerations and orders that can be made in specific areas of family law. However, commonly, one of the reasons why the inherent jurisdiction is often sought is to obtain Tipstaff orders and disclosure orders.

CHAPTER FOUR

THE INHERENT JURISDICTION AND CHILD ABDUCTION

Introduction

The inherent jurisdiction is often known for its use in cases of child abduction. This child abduction can take two forms, abduction from England and Wales to a non-Hague state, or secondly, an abduction from a non-Hague state to England and Wales. These two scenarios engage the inherent jurisdiction of the High Court. This chapter will explore the role of the inherent jurisdiction in cases relating to child abduction or risk of child abduction.

Why the inherent jurisdiction

The first question is, why does the inherent jurisdiction need to be exercised in cases of child abduction? Firstly, one successfully international treaty is the 1980 Hague Convention. This Convention has a number of signatories, approximately close to 100 countries. The Convention sets out clearly in Article 1 a clear aim:

'The objects of the present Convention are -

a) to secure the prompt return of children wrongfully removed to or retained in any Contracting State; and

b) to ensure that rights of custody and of access under the law of one Contracting State are effectively respected in the other Contracting States'

Further, Article 2 and 11 sets out the need for proceedings under the 1980 Hague Convention to be dealt with expeditiously. Article 2 states:

> *'Contracting States shall take all appropriate measures to secure within their territories the implementation of the objects of the Convention. For this purpose they shall use the most expeditious procedures available'*

Article 11 states:

> *'The judicial or administrative authorities of Contracting States shall act expeditiously in proceedings for the return of children.*
>
> *If the judicial or administrative authority concerned has not reached a decision within six weeks from the date of commencement of the proceedings, the applicant or the Central Authority of the requested State, on its own initiative or if asked by the Central Authority of the requesting State, shall have the right to request a statement of the reasons for the delay. If a reply is received by the Central Authority of the requested State, that Authority shall transmit the reply to the Central Authority of the requesting State, or to the applicant, as the case may be'*

It is therefore apparent from its language; the Convention is a strict treaty with focused aims. It outlined the impact upon child abduction and how states who are signatories to the Convention must act expeditiously in determining a 1980 Hague Convention.

In England, 1980 Hague Convention cases are heard in the High Court also. For example, if a child is abducted from a signatory to the Convention to this country, the proceedings will commence in the High Court and remain there until the conclusion of the proceedings. High Court judges are therefore particularly experienced at dealing with child abduction matters. The provisions are often regarded as being interpreted narrowly because the aim is to return children to the country of their habitual residence. The Convention considers in detail what is regarded as wrongful removal or wrongful retention and what the exceptions to a summary return are. Perhaps the matter can be explained nicely by Mostyn J in B v B[22] where his lordship stated:

> '*2 The Hague Convention of 1980 is arguably the most successful ever international treaty and it has over 90 subscribers to it, over half the countries in the world. The underlying and central foundation of the Convention is that, where a child has been unilaterally removed from the land of her habitual residence in breach of someone's rights of custody, then she should be swiftly returned to that country for the courts of that country to decide on her long*-term future.
>
> *3 There are very few exceptions to this and the exceptions that do exist have to be interpreted very narrowly in order that the central premise of the Convention is not fatally undermined. It is important to understand what the Convention does not do. The Convention does not order a child who has been removed in the circumstances I have described to live with anybody. The Convention does not provide that the parent who is left behind should, on the return of the child, have contact or access in any particular way. The Convention does not provide that, when an order for return to the child's homeland is made, the child should stay there indefinitely. All the Convention provides is that the child should be returned for the specific purpose and limited period to enable the court of her homeland to decide on her long-term future. That is all it decides.*
>
> *4 ... Equally, if the exception that is relied on is that there is a grave risk that his or her return would expose the child to physical or psychological harm or otherwise place her in an intolerable situation, that again has to be seen through the lens of the objective of the Convention. We are not talking here about long- term risks. We are not talking here about long-term harm. We are talking about risks and harm that would eventuate only in the period that it takes for the court*

22 [2014] EWHC 1804

of the child's homeland to determine her long-term future and to impose the necessary safeguards, if necessary, in the interim.'

Further in Re D (A Child) (Abduction: Rights of Custody)[23], Baroness Hale of Richmond observed:

'The whole object of the Convention is to secure the swift return of children wrongfully removed from their home country, not only so that they can return to the place which is properly their 'home', but also so that any dispute about where they should live in the future can be decided in the courts of their home country, according to the laws of their home country and in accordance with the evidence which will mostly be there rather than in the country to which they have been removed'

This leads onto the issue of the inherent jurisdiction. The reason why the inherent jurisdiction is in place is because many countries are not signatories to the 1980 Hague Convention. Despite the positive words of the 1980 Hague Convention by the highest level of judges in England, and also judges in other signatory countries, some countries have still not signed up to. Therefore, if a child abduction takes place from or two a non-Hague state, the only mechanism a party can utilise is the inherent jurisdiction.

Abduction and the Inherent Jurisdiction – General Principles

The next headings in this chapter will consider inward and outward abductions. However, before this, it is important to outline the leading case relating to inherent jurisdiction proceedings. That is Re NY (A Child)[24]. This case outlined the principle that if a party is seeking a return

[23] [2006] UKLH 51, para 48

[24] [2019] UKSC 49

order through the inherent jurisdiction, then the point of reference for the court is the subject child's welfare.

The Supreme court set out 8 principles. These 8 points are what practitioners need to have in mind for any inward or outward abduction case. Each principle will have an impact upon the timetable and therefore must be grappled with urgently. Inward and outward abduction proceedings are 'summary' and therefore an applicant should ensure in particular, that the proceedings are timetabled and each of the below are considered:

> '*55. I respectfully suggest, however, that, before making a summary order under the inherent jurisdiction for this child to be returned to Israel, the Court of Appeal should have given (but did not give) at least some consideration to eight further, linked, questions.*
>
> *56. First, the court, which was sitting on 18 June 2019, should have considered whether the evidence before it was sufficiently up to date to enable it then to make the summary order. The mother's statement in answer to the claim under the Convention was dated 29 March 2019. In it she had devoted seven out of 67 paragraphs to assertions of the child's habitual residence in England and of particular circumstances said to demonstrate how happy and settled she had become. In his statement in reply dated 11 April the father had joined issue with the mother's assertions. The oral evidence given by the parties to the judge on 15 April had been limited to the issue of consent to the child's removal from Israel and so had not addressed these matters.*
>
> *57. Second, the court should have considered whether the judge had made, or whether it could make, findings sufficient to justify the summary order. The only relevant finding made by the judge had been that on 10 January 2019, only seven weeks after her arrival in England, the child had retained habitual residence in Israel. Was that sufficient to justify the making of a summary order five months later? In the light of the policy in favour of the making of substantive welfare determinations by the courts of habitual residence, did there need to be*

inquiry into the child's habitual residence at the relevant date, which, in the absence of an application, was in this case the date of the proposed order?

58. Third, the court should have considered whether, in order sufficiently to identify what the child's welfare required for the purposes of a summary order, an inquiry should be conducted into any or all of the aspects of welfare specified in section 1(3) of the 1989 Act and, if so, how extensive that inquiry should be: see para 49 above. It might in particular have considered that the third of those aspects, namely "the likely effect on [the child] of any change in [her] circumstances", merited inquiry.

59. Fourth, the court should have considered whether in the light of Practice Direction 12J, an inquiry should be conducted into the disputed allegations made by the mother of domestic abuse and, if so, how extensive that inquiry should be: see para 50 above. The judge had made no findings about them. Instead, in accordance with the E case cited in para 12 above, he had, for the purposes of the claim under the Convention, made a reasonable assumption in relation to the maximum level of risk to the child arising out of any domestic abuse to be perpetrated by the father and had considered that such risk would be contained within acceptable limits by undertakings offered by the father, the enforceability of which in Israel the judge had not explored. Consideration should therefore have been given to whether, in a determination to be governed by the child's welfare, the judge's approach to the mother's allegations remained sufficient.

60. Fifth, the court should have considered whether, without identification in evidence of any arrangements for the child in Israel, in particular of where she and the mother would live, it would be appropriate to conclude that her welfare required her to return there.

61. Sixth, the court should have considered whether, in the light of its consideration of the five matters identified above, any oral evidence should be given by the parties and, if so, upon what aspects and to what extent.

62. Seventh, the court should have considered whether, in the light of its consideration of the same matters, a CAFCASS officer should be directed to prepare a report and, if so, upon what aspects and to what extent. It is noteworthy that in the L case discussed in para 43 above, a CAFCASS report had been prepared. It had been designed to ascertain the boy's wishes and feelings and so was apparently made as if pursuant to section 1(3)(a) of the 1989 Act: see para 14 of Baroness Hale's judgment. In her careful weighing, in paras 34 to 37 of her judgment, of the welfare considerations which militated both in favour of, and against, the boy's return to Texas, Baroness Hale relied to a significant extent upon the content of the CAFCASS report.

63. Eighth, the court should have considered whether it needed to compare the relative abilities of the Rabbinical Court in Jerusalem and the Family Court in London to reach a swift resolution of the substantive issues between the parents in relation to the child and to satisfy itself that the Rabbinical Court had power to authorise the mother to relocate with the child back to England: see para 34 above.

64. The effect of the above is not to submerge efficient exercise of the inherent jurisdiction to make a summary order within an ocean of onerous judicial obligations. The linked obligations are obligations only to consider the eight specified matters. There is no need for us to contemplate what the proper outcome of the Court of Appeal's consideration of them might have been. It is the fact that it failed even to consider them which yields the conclusion that it conducted no defensible analysis of the child's welfare prior to its determination to make the summary order and which led this court to uphold the mother's appeal'.

Accordingly, issues relating to PD12J, Cafcass, evidence generally relating to welfare is crucial. How these factors are considered can alter the timetable. If there needs to be a fact-finding, then this will create a delay. A welfare assessment is likely to be ordered only after a fact-finding hearing. Alternatively, if the matter only requires a welfare enquiry, then it should be noted that the paramountcy of the subject child's welfare may not necessarily require a full welfare enquiry. Each case is fact specific. Practitioners should have the 8 principles in consideration always during inherent jurisdiction cases particularly in cases relating to child abduction.

Inward Abduction

It is important practitioners are alive to two possibilities here:

A. The country where the children were abducted is a non-Hague state; or

B. The country where the children were abducted from, is a Hague state, but the inherent jurisdiction needs to be utilised.

In respect of point B, there are circumstances where the 1980 Hague Convention does not apply. For example, if the return is for a child over the aged of 16[25] and therefore the Convention does not apply. In these circumstances, the issue is that of welfare under the inherent jurisdiction. As outlined in Re J (Child Returned Abroad: Convention Rights)[26]

> *'in all non-Convention cases, the courts have consistently held that they must act in accordance with the welfare of the individual child. If they do decide to return the child, that is because it is in his best interests to do so, not because the welfare principle has been superseded by some other consideration'*

25 Re Q (Children) (1980 Hague Convention: Inherent Jurisdiction Summary Return) [2019] EWHC 490 (Fam) also see Article 4 of the 1980 Hague Convention

26 [2005] 2 FLR 802, at paragraph 25

Further, Re J makes clear there is a choice before the Court: '*it is plain, therefore, that there is always a choice to be made. Summary return should not be the automatic reaction to any and every unauthorised taking or keeping a child from his home country. On the other hand, summary return may very well be in the best interests of the individual child*'[27]

Moreover, as Baroness Hale stated in Re J, the following:

> '*The most one can say, in my view, is that the judge may find it convenient to start from the proposition that it is likely to be better for a child to return to his home country for any disputes about his future to be decided there. A case against his doing so has to be made. But the weight to be given to that proposition will vary enormously from case to case. What may be best for him in the long run may be different from what will be best for him in the short run. It should not be assumed, in this or any other case, that allowing a child to remain here while his future is decided here inevitably means that he will remain here for ever*'[28]

The above is a position. It is not a presumption and therefore depending upon the facts of a case, the issue can be grappled with.

Accordingly, an assessment is that of Children Act 1989 and welfare. In circumstances where there is clearly an international case in existence, there has been a vast amount of case law considering the issue. Therefore, points such as the connection the child has to each competing country[29] the child's views, the legal systems available in each country for example. There will be a broad assessment and in circumstances where a respondent seeks to defend a summary return application, they need to consider having a Cafcass assessment in respect of welfare. Welfare is the

---

27 Paragraph 28

28 Paragraph 32

29 Re L (Minors) (Wardship: Jurisdiction) [1974] 1 WLR 250

key concept and as described by Lord Donaldson MR in Re F (Minor) (Abduction: Jurisdiction)[30]:

> *'The welfare of the child is indeed the paramount consideration, but it has to be considered in two different contexts. The first is the context of which court shall decide what the child's best interests require. The second context, which only arises if it has first been decided that the welfare of the child requires that the English rather than a foreign court shall decide what are the requirements of the child, is what orders as to custody, care and control and so on, should be made.'*

Equally, in respect of any points relating to the legal system, there should be a consideration of a Part25 expert to address the issue. The case of LM v DR[31] demonstrates the issue. The party resisting a summary return will have to demonstrate that the issue of the legal system in that country is relevant to the welfare of the child in circumstances where a return order is resisted.

Another consideration is the voice of the child. Just like 1980 Hague Convention cases, there is a vast number of reported decisions on the issue. Afterall, when the issue is that of welfare, the child's views are going to be a consideration within the checklist of factors and could ultimately, be a key one at that Practitioners should address this at the first case management hearing. Cafcass should be contacted in order to obtain their timescales to do a report as well as the remit of the report. As outlined earlier, a full welfare assessment may not be necessary and therefore the timing for the report to be completed may differ. The scope of the report should be addresses at the first hearing and recorded clearly in the report.

---

30 [1991] 1 FLR 1

31 [2016] EWHC 1943 (Fam)

In terms of the essential nature of the child's voice, the Court of Appeal in Re S (A Child)[32] outlines the following international obligations:

'[15] Article 12 of the United Nations Convention on the Rights of the Child 1989 [UNCRC] provides that:

'1. States parties shall assure to the child who is capable of forming his or her own views the right to express those views freely in all matters affecting the child, the views of the child being given due weight in accordance with the age and maturity of the child.

2. For this purpose, the child shall in particular be provided the opportunity to be heard in any judicial and administrative proceedings affecting the child, either directly, or through a representative or an appropriate body, in a manner consistent with the procedural rules of national law."

[16] The UNCRC creates international obligations rather than domestic rights. That said, it is consistent with and has a persuasive interpretative effect on other international instruments that are binding on the United Kingdom. For example, art 24 of the Charter of Fundamental Rights of the European Union provides that:

"1. Children shall have the right to such protection and care as is necessary for their well being. They may express their views freely. Such views shall be taken into consideration on matters which concern them in accordance with their age and maturity.

2. In all actions relating to children, whether taken by public authorities or private institutions, the child's best interests must be a primary consideration.'

32 (Abduction: Hearing the Child) [2014] EWCA Civ 1557

The 1980 Hague Convention would also not apply if the applicant cannot prove rights of custody immediately prior to the retention nor removal pursuant to Article 3[33].

Outward Abduction

Proceedings relating to outward abductions tend to be more difficult to progress and timetable and require practitioners to think strategically from the outset of proceedings. This is because, in circumstances where a respondent has abducted a child to a non-Hague state, then a number of practical obstacles arise and can materialise. Firstly, the action of the respondent to take a child to a non-Hague state within itself is a problem. The non-Hague state has no bilateral agreement with the Courts of England and Wales and therefore the respondent may be seeking to evade justice. Other issues that often arise in this case:

A. Whether to go without notice or not;

B. Any assistance that can be obtained from agencies / government bodies;

C. Tracing and locating the respondent / child;

D. Ensuring the respondent engages with the proceedings;

E. Enabling the child's voice to be heard; and

F. Ensuring compliance.

Whether to go without notice or not

As outlined earlier, there are very limited circumstances where the need to go without notice is necessary. It would be fair to say, an abduction to a non-Hague state is an urgent one and a scenario where it would be

33 Re W (Abduction: Father's Rights) [998] 2 FLR 146

appropriate to go without notice. This is for a number of reasons. Often, the precise factual basis is not clear at the beginning, for example, whether the respondent intends to return back or not or the purpose of travel or even the location of travel. Accordingly, an applicant will instantly be thinking about Tipstaff orders. This would enable port alerts to be enacted in the event the respondent travels back to England. This would be sought on a without notice hearing because if the respondent was alerted to such an order, the respondent may actively choose not to return back. Often in these types of cases, it is only when the port alert bites and the respondents travel documents are then seised upon a return to England can progress be made. Everything needs to be done to ensure the respondent returns back, with or without the children to enable the respondent to be forced to engage with the proceedings.

How long the proceedings have to be without notice is another question. Often, many hearings are without notice in order to ascertain information. The applicant would need to utilise the inherent jurisdiction to obtain disclosure orders to try and ascertain as much information as possible. For example, disclosure orders could reveal where the respondent is depositing / withdrawing money (if using a UK bank account), or when and where they left too. From this point onwards, orders can be made and humble requests of the High Court to the embassy of that county to assist.

Eventually, it will be necessary to order the respondent to attend the proceedings and engage. This does not mean the respondent should be provided with the full disclosure of the without notice material. It is the opposite. You would want the respondent to engage in proceedings but not be aware of the true position in that the applicant and the court may have a vast amount of information available as to the respondent's location.

Another reason why proceedings may be without notice for a while is that the respondent may decide to simply not engage in the proceedings and feel safe within a non-Hague state. In these circumstances, the pressure will shift onto whatever action needs to be taken to secure the return of the children. This could involve orders against family members, freezing orders / injunctions against the respondent's assets (including bank accounts / homes), sequestration of assets etc. The purpose is to take every step necessary in order to create as much pressure on the respondent to engage within proceedings. Ultimately, the applicant may have no choice but to commence contempt of court proceedings (which will be considered later).

<u>Any assistance that can be obtained from agencies / government bodies</u>

Child Abduction is a criminal offence in England and Wales. In parallel to family law proceedings, pressure can be inserted upon the police and the Crown Prosecution Service to take relevant action. If a finding is obtained in inherent jurisdiction proceedings that someone abducted a child, then the applicant may seek for the police to up their efforts and to obtain arrest warrants with Interpol notices. Therefore, disclosure of important orders / judgments to the police in England must be a step the applicant's legal representatives think about.

Further, in circumstances where it is known that the respondent and child is in another country, orders disclosed to relevant embassy's / government bodies may be of assistance. This is a common occurrence in outward abduction cases within the inherent jurisdiction. A useful example as reported is that of Singer J in Re KR (Abduction: forcible removal by parents)[34] where the following helpful wording was outlined and set out in the judgment:

> *'As a result of that hearing there was drawn an order which I hoped would have some extra-territorial effect, in the sense that it might encourage relevant authorities in India to give assistance. I have been informed that it did indeed have that effect, and in the hope that in*

[34] [1999] 2 FLR 542, at 546

comparable situations others may find such an order of assistance, I now reproduce its essential terms:

'UPON hearing …

AND UPON the application of all parties herein and by consent of all parties herein and upon reading … and upon hearing …

AND WHEREAS KR is a ward of this honourable court and is a British citizen; born in and domiciled in the UK; and currently travelling with a UK passport

AND WHEREAS in consequence of the fact that this court has ordered that KR remain a ward of this court while (until she attains the age of 18 years on [date]) she remains a minor, this court is empowered and required to exercise its custodial jurisdiction over her and to ascertain her best interests and to facilitate and protect those best interests

AND WHEREAS this honourable court is anxious to protect and secure her well-being and best interests and to ensure that she may freely express her wishes concerning her country and place of residence

AND WHEREAS this honourable court is anxious to ensure that she is not induced or coerced into contracting any marriage or betrothal against her will

AND WHEREAS this honourable court is satisfied that all interested parties are before the court including the Official Solicitor appointed by the court to represent the ward

AND WHEREAS this honourable court having heard limited oral evidence from [F and M] is of the view that serious grounds exist in the present circumstances to question whether this honourable court's ward KR is able freely to express her views and wishes and in particular with regard to her country of residence

> *IT IS ORDERED that every person in a position to do so shall co-operate in assisting and securing the immediate return to England of KR, a ward of this honourable court*
>
> *AND NOW THEREFORE this court invites all judicial and administrative bodies in the State of India to render assistance in establishing the whereabouts of the ward of this honourable court and in arranging for her to be placed in contact with the British High Commission in New Delhi (Reference: [a named individual]) and to facilitate her travel to the British High Commission with a view to her immediate return to the UK."*

Such wording in the order can have some persuasive effect when the court and the parties to a case maybe reliant upon authorities assisting. As recognised by Hogg J in Re S (Wardship: Stranded Spouses):[35]

> '*Given the international element and the experience of the judges of the Family Division in dealing with cases of this type, child abduction and other international cases, the best vehicle for these type of cases is wardship...*'

Tracing and locating the respondent / child;

This ties in with the ex-parte heading above. It is a sad reality that a respondent could abduct children to a non-Hague state they either are from, or to where they have no existing links. It can be difficult to locate a respondent in the first place. Nonetheless, upon Tipstaff orders being made, Tipstaff can undertake an international movement check. This will outline the date and time the children and respondent travelled and to where to. Once this is located, then requests can be made to the country for assistance in providing information. Of course, there may be nothing stopping the respondent from leaving one country to another and then this is where the difficulty materialises.

---

35 [2010] EWHC 1669 (Fam), para 1

Alternatively, disclosure orders against bank accounts and phone record companies may be able to help in finding where the respondent is. Additionally, attendance orders against close family members of the respondent (who are still in England) for them to attend the High Court and give evidence on oath about any information they know is also an option.

Ensuring the respondent engages with the proceedings

Orders can be made against a respondent even if they are in a non-Hague state. These orders should contain a penal notice and so the respondent is aware of the consequences of breaching any orders. There is a risk the respondent does not engage with proceedings. The applicant must be proportionate about strategy and to ensure each stage of proceedings are conducted fairly, if the respondent is attending. This would enable the court to determine the issues fairly and openly and the respondent can be satisfied about the process embarked upon.

Moreover, if a respondent chooses to return back to England despite the outward abduction, then the applicant may seek to enter into undertakings. These undertakings can be described as soft-landing provisions to reassure the respondent that upon their return, certain action will not be taken. For example, not to 'voluntarily supporting punishment via the criminal or civil courts as a consequence of the wrongful removal' or to not 'separate the children from the respondent until the matter is considered at the first inter partes hearing'. The undertakings can also provide other matters, such as funding the flights for the respondent and children to return or to provide them for temporary accommodation. This must be considered to reassure the respondent to return back to England.

Enabling the child's voice to be heard

The Cafcass High Court team are experienced at dealing with international child abduction cases. However, it has to be noted that in circumstances where a child is outside the jurisdiction of England, then the job is invariably harder and can present with a number of practical obstacles. For example, it can be difficult for the child to be spoken to on a video call, or to observe indirect contact. The welfare assessment is therefore likely to be difficult and this is something that parties have to consider. Within the court order there should be clear expectations about how the child must be made available to speak to Cafcass as well as the timings and dates to be confirmed. It is likely a welfare report is likely to be of limited nature until the child is returned to England.

Ensuring compliance

As indicated, a respondent in a non-Hague state may not comply with return orders or engage with proceedings. In such circumstances, the applicant may have no choice but to explore every possible avenue including the freezing of assets. Alternatively, to pursue a contempt of court application. The rules of which are complicated in nature.

The rules relating to committal appear in FPR 2010. r.37.2. This rule sets out a number of definitions:

> *'contempt application" means an application to the court for an order determining contempt proceedings;*
>
> *"order of committal" means the imposition of a sentence of imprisonment (whether immediate or suspended) for contempt of court;*
>
> *"penal notice" means a prominent notice on the front of an order warning that if the person against whom the order is made (and, in the case of a corporate body, a director or officer of that body) disobeys the court's order, the person (or director or officer) may be held in contempt of court and punished by a fine, imprisonment, confiscation of assets or other punishment under the law'*

Rule 37.4(1) sets out that unless and to the extent that the court directs otherwise, every contempt application must be supported by written evidence given by affidavit or affirmation. Rule 37.4(2) contains information as to what must be included in such an application. Rule .37.8(1) states all hearings of contempt proceedings shall be listed and heard in public unless the court directs otherwise.

If there are any procedural defects in any application, then the court does have the ability in accordance PD 37A para 2(2):

> '*(2) The court may waive any procedural defect in the commencement or conduct of a contempt application if satisfied that no injustice has been caused to the defendant by the defect.*'

Effecting Service

In outward abduction cases, the issue of service is one that can be tricky to effect if the respondent is in another jurisdiction, then it can be virtually impossible to prove personal service. There are alternatives to personal service (it is clear from case law that the court may order service out of the jurisdiction by an alternative method: Wilmot v Maughan[36]. However, practitioners should seek to deal with this issue before the issue materialises. Where the respondent is required to do something, the same court order should set out the method of service the court specifically approves. For example, wording in the order can include something like 'personal service is dispensed with, providing the documents are sent to the respondent via email'. A practical example appears in in Emoni v Atabo[37] [Lieven J DBE when considering the issue of service in light of the particular facts of that case outlined:

> '*The order provided for service by email given that personal service is extremely difficult to effect in Lagos. The relevant email address is one that has been used by her on a number of occasions and on which she has had no difficulty receiving emails. The Order of 2 November 2020*

---

36 [2018 1 FLR 1306, CA

37 [2020] EWHC 3322

> *was sent to that email address by the court on 3 November 2020 and all relevant documents were sent to that email address. In light of that history I have no doubt she has been properly served with documents including the notice of today's hearing*

Another point practitioners should have in mind, is to ensure that not only the orders are drafted clearly, but penal notices appear in them. For example, in Egeneonu v Egeneonu [38]David Williams QC (as he then was) sitting as a Deputy Judge of the High Court, gave some helpful guidance at paragraph 21:

> *'To have penal consequences, an order needs to be clear on its face as to precisely what it means and precisely what it prohibits or requires to be done. Contempt will not be established where the breach is of an order which is ambiguous, or which does not require or forbid the performance of a particular act within a specified timeframe. The person or persons affected must know with complete precision what it is that they are required to do or abstain from doing. It is not possible to imply terms into an injunction. The first task for the judge hearing an application for committal for alleged breach of a mandatory (positive) order is to identify, by reference to the express language of the order, precisely what it is that the order required the defendant to do. That is a question of construction and, thus, a question of law.'*

And :

> *'Contempt of court involves a contumelious that is to say a deliberate, disobedience to the order. If it be the case that the accused cannot comply with order then he is not in contempt of court. It is not enough to suspect recalcitrance. It is for the applicant to establish that it was within the power of the defendant to do what the order required. It is not for the defendant to establish that it was not within his power to do it. That burden remains on the applicant throughout but it does*

---

38 [2017] EWHC 2336 (Fam)

not require the applicant to adduce evidence of a particular means of compliance which was available to the accused provided the applicant can satisfy the judge so that he is sure that compliance was possible.'

Respondent Not in Attendance?

There may be a situation where a committal application is pursued but the respondent does not attend. If the respondent is in another jurisdiction the question as to whether committal should be pursued is a key one. The question practitioners should seek to answer is, would a committal application achieve much? If the respondent is aware the court has imprisoned him in England and Wales, it is questionable whether the respondent has any incentive to comply with court orders and to return to England and Wales, because if the respondent did return, they should be arrested. Notwithstanding this possibility, there are circumstances where applicant have pursued committal applications. This is because perhaps all avenues have been explored / pursued in England and Wales and there is no choice but to pursue a committal. A benefit of committal proceedings in this sense is that the judgment is usually published in a form which is not anonymised. This is because the hearing is conducted in public. This can generate public interest in a case and can put pressure on the respondent to comply with orders and return because there is media attention in respect of their actions.

In the event an applicant wishes to pursue an application for committal where the respondent is not in attendance, there are further obstacles the court must assess.

Mr Justice Cobb considered such a scenario in Sanchez v Pawell Oboz and Jolant Oboz[39] and at paragraph 4 he said this:

[39] [2015] EWHC 235 (Fam)

'It will be an unusual, but by no means exceptional, course to proceed to determine a committal application in the absence of a respondent. This is so because:

i) Committal proceedings are essentially criminal in nature, even if not classified in our national law as such (see Benham v United Kingdom (1996) 22 EHRR 293 at [56], Ravnsborg v. Sweden (1994), Series A no. 283-B); in a criminal context, proceeding with a trial in the absence of the accused is a course which will be followed only with great caution, and with close regard to the fairness of the proceedings (see R v Jones (Anthony) [2003] 1 AC 1, approving the checklist provided in R v Jones; R v Purvis [2001] QB 862);

ii) Findings of fact are required before any penalty can be considered in committal proceedings; the presumption of innocence applies (Article 6(2) ECHR). The tribunal of fact is generally likely to be at a disadvantage in determining the relevant facts in the absence of a party;

iii) The penalty of imprisonment for a proven breach of an order is one of the most significant powers of a judge exercising the civil/family jurisdiction; the respondent faces the real prospect of a deprivation of liberty;

iv) By virtue of the quasi-criminal nature of committal process, Article 6(1) and Article 6(3) ECHR are actively engaged (see Re K (Contact: Committal Order) [2002] EWCA Civ 1559, [2003] 1 FLR 277 and Begum v Anam [2004] EWCA Civ 578); Article 6(1) entitles the respondent to a "a fair and public hearing"; that hearing is to be "within a reasonable time";

v) Article 6(3) specifically provides for someone in the position of an alleged contemnor "to defend himself in person or through legal assistance of his own choosing", though this is not an absolute right in the sense of "entitling someone necessarily to indefinite offers of legal assistance if they behave so unreasonably as to make it impossible for the funders to continue sensibly to provide legal assistance" (per Mance LJ (as he then was) in Re K (Contact: Committal Order) (reference above)). The respondent is also entitled to "have adequate time and the facilities for the preparation of his defence" (Article 6(3)(b)).'

At paragraph 5, Cobb J further stated:

'As neither respondent has attended this hearing, and in view of Mr. Gration's application to proceed in their absence, I have paid careful attention to the factors identified in [4] above, and, adapting the guidance from R v Jones; R v Purvis, have considered with care the following specific issues:

i) Whether the respondents have been served with the relevant documents, including the notice of this hearing;

ii) Whether the respondents have had sufficient notice to enable them to prepare for the hearing;

iii) Whether any reason has been advanced for their non-appearance;

iv) Whether by reference to the nature and circumstances of the respondents' behaviour, they have waived their right to be present (i.e., is it reasonable to conclude that the respondents knew of, or were indifferent to, the consequences of the case proceeding in their absence);

v) Whether an adjournment for would be likely to secure the attendance of the respondents, or at least facilitate their representation;

vi) The extent of the disadvantage to the respondents in not being able to present their account of events;

vii) Whether undue prejudice would be caused to the applicant by any delay;

viii) Whether undue prejudice would be caused to the forensic process if the application was to proceed in the absence of the respondents;

> *ix) The terms of the 'overriding objective' (rule 1.1 FPR 2010), including the obligation on the court to deal with the case 'justly', including doing so "expeditiously and fairly" (r.1.1(2)), and taking "any … step or make any… order for the purposes of… furthering the overriding objective" (r.4.1(3)(o))'*

It is therefore apparent that when someone's liberty is at stake and committal is being pursued in the absence of the party, the court has to be satisfied various obstacles have been overcome to enable the hair to be fair in the particular circumstances. Further recent case law in respect of committal hearings can be found in: Addou v Bennabi[40] which is an outward return case. Further, the Court of Appeal and MacDonald J considered and applied contempt of court principles in Allami v Faker[41].

Conclusion

This chapter outlines the use of the inherent jurisdiction in child abduction cases. The ultimate aim is to prevent abduction through the use of the inherent jurisdiction or alternatively, to secure a child's return back to this country following child abduction. The inherent jurisdiction has many powers to assist in achieving both goals. Putting the return aside, there is also a number of orders and powers that practitioners must be alive to in trying to do whatever it takes to secure compliance before the decision to escalate matters is taken

40 [2022] EWHC 3146

41 [2023] EWFC 59 and in the Court of Appeal, [2023] EWCA 532

CHAPTER FIVE

THE INHERENT JURISDICTION AND PUBLIC LAW PROCEEDINGS

Introduction

This Chapter will consider the ways in which the state can seek to use the provision of the inherent jurisdiction. Typically, 'public law' proceedings are regarded as proceedings where the local authority seek a public law order, such an interim care order or interim supervision order. This chapter will consider 'public law' in the wider sense, to consider example the variety of ways in which in which the local authority, through their social work department may seek use of the inherent jurisdiction in particular circumstances, often in cases of great urgency or where there is a real risk of harm in existence. However, we will be outlined in this chapter there are statutory limitations on restricting the local authority's use of inherent jurisdiction and wardship.

The Inherent Jurisdiction and the Local Authority

The benefit of the inherent jurisdiction of the High Court is that it arises for a local authority in circumstances where other remedies under the Children Act 1989 are non-existent. In contrast, there may be provisions contained within statute, namely the Children Act 1989 which does not warrant the local authority seeking relief through the inherent jurisdiction. Accordingly, there is a vast amount of case law dealing with the issue and outlining what relief a local authority can seek in the context of protecting children, whether in the middle of public law proceedings or not.

At the outset it must be outlined that there are many cases that can be dealt with and managed by High Court judges sitting in the High Court. This does not mean that the inherent jurisdiction is being exercised. For example, in public law proceedings where there are complex proceedings relating to medical evidence or a child's death[42] there may be lengthy fact-finding hearings. These are heard by a High Court judge due to the complexity in existence, not because the inherent jurisdiction is being invoked.

<u>The inherent jurisdiction verses the Children Act 1989</u>

As already indicated, if statue exists for the local authority to seek a particular relief, then it is not open for them to seek it through the inherent jurisdiction. The wording to this effect can be found within the Children Act 1989, namely Section 100 (2) which states:

> *'(2) No court shall exercise the High Court's inherent jurisdiction with respect to children—*
>
> *(a) so as to require a child to be placed in the care, or put under the supervision, of a local authority;*
>
> *(b) so as to require a child to be accommodated by or on behalf of a local authority;*
>
> *(c) so as to make a child who is the subject of a care order a ward of court; or*
>
> *(d) for the purpose of conferring on any local authority power to determine any question which has arisen, or which may arise, in connection with any aspect of parental responsibility for a child.*

---

42 For example, see London Borough of Southward v A Family [2020] EWHC 3117

(3) No application for any exercise of the court's inherent jurisdiction with respect to children may be made by a local authority unless the authority have obtained the leave of the court.

(4) The court may only grant leave if it is satisfied that—

(a) the result which the authority wish to achieve could not be achieved through the making of any order of a kind to which subsection (5) applies; and

(b) there is reasonable cause to believe that if the court's inherent jurisdiction is not exercised with respect to the child he is likely to suffer significant harm.

(5) This subsection applies to any order—

(a) made otherwise than in the exercise of the court's inherent jurisdiction; and

(b) which the local authority is entitled to apply for (assuming, in the case of any application which may only be made with leave, that leave is granted)'

In contrast, it can therefore be thought that the inherent jurisdiction is a useful mechanism to utilise to safeguard children when other procedures and remedies were unavailable, or had failed.

Therefore, in circumstances where an interim care order or care order exists, the local authority already has parental responsibility. Therefore, they are able to exercise parental responsibility. However, some questions do arise as to when the inherent jurisdiction will be applicable or not.

In terms therefore of invoking the inherent jurisdiction for a local authority, a summary of why statute may not always be there to provide the necessary safeguards can be outlined in the Supreme Court in Re T[43]:

> *'the inherent jurisdiction has had to rise to the challenge of some of the most extreme human and moral dilemmas imaginable, a notable example of this in relatively recent times being In re A (Children) (Conjoined Twins: Surgical Separation) [2001] Fam 147. As Lord Donaldson of Lymington MR said in In re F (Mental Patient: Sterilisation) [1990] 2 AC 1, p 13 (in a passage approved by the House of Lords on appeal):*
>
> *"the common law is the great safety net which lies behind all statute law and is capable of filling gaps left by that law, if and in so far as those gaps have to be filled in the interests of society as a whole. This process of using the common law to fill gaps is one of the most important duties of the judges'*

There are therefore some situations where a local authority may therefore need to exercise the inherent jurisdiction which will be considered in this chapter.

Duties of the Local Authority

It is worth noting that the Local Authority have a number of duties which is enshrined in statute. Part III of the Children Act 1989, which is entitled '*Support for Children and Families Provided by Local Authorities in England*'. It covers, the provision of services for children in need and their families, the provision of accommodation for children and the duties of local authorities in relation to children that are to be said to be looked after by them.

Section 20 of the Act creates the duty in respect of accommodation for any child in need within the local authority's area who appears to require

43 (A Child) [2021] UKSC 35, paragraph 67

accommodation because no one has parental responsibility for the child, or instead, because the child is lost or abandoned, or because the person who has been caring for the child is prevented from providing with suitable accommodation or care. Section 22G deals with the general duty of a local authority to take steps to secure, 'so far as reasonably practicable', that they are able to provide accommodation needed for children within their area. Section 22 deals specifically with the duties of local authorities in relation to those children who are 'looked after' by them (as defined in section 22(1)). Further, Section 22(3) obliges the local authority to safeguard and promote the welfare of any child they are looking after, and it is worth noting that, by section 22(3A), this includes a duty to promote the child's educational achievement. Section 100 (2) sets out the framework the local authority must consider, as should parents to proceedings in the event the application is challenged. Even if the court is of the view that the inherent jurisdiction can be utilised, the next question is as Sir James Munby once put it: '*Quite plainly I should exercise my powers under the inherent jurisdiction. The questions was, can I and if so how?*'[44]

Child Abduction

The local authority can be involved in proceedings relating to child abduction and may be the main applicant. For example, a child under their care through an interim care order or interim supervision order may be missing. This could be as a result of child abduction and a respondent parent, or both are involved in this. The local authority is able in these circumstances able to urgently apply to the High Court for Tipstaff orders such as a location order or passport order. Further, they could also apply for a collection order. This is all predicated on the basis the Court gives the local authority leave, which ordinarily will not be a problem in the context of existing public law proceedings where it is likely the local

44 Re M (Children) [2015] EWCA 1433, paragraph 27.

family court have made a finding in respect of interim threshold and the issue as to the necessity of local authority protection is already made out.

Under this heading of child abduction in the context of a local authority involvement, the reality is two scenarios can be predicted as to the need to utilise inherent jurisdiction:

a) A child has been abducted already; or

b) There is a risk of abduction.

In terms of a child already being abducted, a useful case example is a case of Bodey J in Lewisham London Borough Council v D[45] His lordship considered an application by a local authority, pursuant to Section100, for leave to seek an order under inherent jurisdiction for the return of a child who is the subject of an interim care order to this jurisdiction and who had been take to Gambia. Considering the provisions of Section 100, his lordship stated at paragraph 30:

> *'Is there any remedy other than the inherent jurisdiction open to the local authority? The only other section which has been considered in argument for recovering T is s 50 of the Children Act 1989, which provides for the 'recovery of abducted children'. However that section contains powers which suggest it is not intended to operate extra-territorially; for example, authorising the removal of a child from wherever he or she may be, and authorising a constable to enter premises. Such types of authority would clearly be outside the gift of the English court in respect of a child in a foreign country. In the result, no one has sought to argue that s 50 would avail the local authority here in trying to recover T, a decision with which I agree'.*

---

[45] (Criteria for Territorial Jurisdiction in Public Law Proceedings) [2008] 2 FLR 1449.

Turning to the second criteria, and on the basis of the facts, his lordship commented:

> *'I turn to the second of the two conditions for leave referred to in s 100(4): is there reasonable cause to believe that T is likely to suffer significant harm if the court's inherent jurisdiction is not exercised? It is right to say that the only psychiatric evidence about the mother is a short report by Dr Rehman (dated 22 July 2005). This is because the mother has declined to engage in the psychiatric assessment which she and the father were offered earlier this year. Dr Rehman then (2005) found the mother not to be 'sectionable' and he felt that her beliefs in black magic might be either explicable in the cultural context, or else due to underlying psychotic illness. He considered that she may need to be reviewed more regularly so as to monitor her mental health; but he did not feel (at that time) that the children were at direct risk of neglect or harm from her. That report, however, was made before a further apparent deterioration in the mother's mental state prior to her departure to The Gambia in April 2007, about which Miss Slater spoke in her evidence, which evidence I accept.*
>
> *[32] I bear in mind The Gambian social services report of Miss Jahateh, dated 2 April 2007, when T was found being looked after by KF and appeared well and seemingly content. The recommendation of Miss Jahateh was that the placement with KF was 'appropriate* in the short term only' *[emphasis added] and that T should be returned in due course to this country. That report was prepared just* before *the mother went out to The Gambia on 13 April 2007, apparently to live in the same house or in the same complex as KF. Since then, there is no evidence as to T's welfare, nor as to the extent to which the mother is in daily contact with her; the father himself is unsure. The court is therefore left in the position of having to do the best it can.*
>
> *[33] I am guided by the speech of Lord Nicholls of Birkenhead in* Re H (Minors) (Sexual Abuse: Standard of Proof) *[1996] AC 563, [1996] 2 WLR 8, [1996] 1 FLR 80 at 583–584, 21–22 and 94D–*

95E respectively. There he said in respect of s 31(2)(a) of the Act (and the same would be applicable to s 100(4)(b)), that the word 'likely' in the expression 'likely to suffer significant harm' is being used '... in the sense of a real possibility, a possibility that cannot sensibly be ignored having regard to the nature and gravity of the feared harm in the particular place'. Referring back to my main judgment for the full details of the mother's delusional beliefs, it can be seen that those beliefs were serious and could well have given rise to (further) serious harm to children in her care. There is no evidence that she has had any psychiatric treatment or assessment since Dr Rehman assessed her relatively briefly in 2005. Although she has instructed counsel, she has not complied with an order of the court that she file evidence. There is no warrant for assuming that her mental state is now any better than it was previously, and all the expert evidence at this hearing (psychiatric and social work) expressed concern at T or any child being in close proximity to her.

[34] In these circumstances, I am persuaded that s 100(4)(b) of the Act is made out. It follows that s 100 is satisfied in full, thus enabling me to give the local authority leave, which I do, to invoke the inherent jurisdiction of the High Court to seek a 'return order'

In contrast, Baker J in SA (A Child)[46] considered a case where a local authority did not have an interim care order and therefore no parental responsibility. His lordship outlined his analysis and the problems with the local authority case at paragraph 11 onwards and stated:

'11 In the case of Lewisham London Borough Council v D (Criteria for Territorial *Jurisdiction* in Public Law Proceedings) [2008] 2 FLR 1449 *Bodey J considered an application by a local authority, pursuant to s.100, for leave to seek an order under inherent jurisdiction for the return of a child who is the subject of an interim care order to this jurisdiction and who had been take to Gambia. The learned judge*

[46] (inherent Jurisdiction: local authority) [2015] EWHC 3997 (Fam)

granted the local authority leave to invoke the jurisdiction. In that case the local authority had parental responsibility for the child by reason of the interim order. Bodey J observed that the effect of an order under inherent jurisdiction for the return of the child to this country would not be placing the child within the care of the local authority, thereby falling foul of s.100(2)(a), but rather would be "to supplement the current interim care order and to make it efficacious".

12 In that case, of course, the local authority had parental responsibility under an interim care order. In contrast, in the current case the local authority does not have parental responsibility, nor does it seek an interim care order in respect of S for the reasons spelt out above. The question arises, therefore, as to whether a local authority can request the High Court, under its inherent jurisdiction, to order the return of a child when it does not have, nor seek, parental responsibility, but merely seeks the return of the child from this jurisdiction for the purposes of pursuing the proceedings.

13 On behalf of the guardian, Mr. Lock suggests that it would be open to the local authority to seek to invoke the jurisdiction of the High Court, assuming it is granted leave to do so, under s.100 (3) for these reasons: first, he submits that it could be argued that there is reasonable cause to believe that if inherent jurisdiction is not exercised in respect of the child she is likely to suffer significant harm; further, that the result which the local authority wishes to achieve could not be achieved other than through inherent jurisdiction of the court. In other words, there is no other order, suggests Mr. Lock, which the local authority could apply for under the Children Act which would enable it to achieve its objective.

14 Here he suggests the child would be at risk of significant harm if not returned, because it could be argued that she would not have the benefit of the support that would be provided under the interim supervision order. On the other hand, it seems to me that in the circumstances of this case it would be open to the local authority to

> *apply for an interim care order, thereby apply parental responsibility and not remove the child from the care of the parents. In other words, it is a care order with the children remaining at home. To that Mr. Lock responds that that would only be achieved if the Placement of Children with Parents Regulations were satisfied.*
>
> *15 Be that as it may, in any event, in the absence of any evidence as to the situation in Saint Kitts, it seems to me to be impossible for the local authority to satisfy me that the test set out in s.100(4)(b) is satisfied, even if Mr. Lock's subtle legal argument is correct. The mother has, on the evidence before me, taken the child to Saint Kitts for a limited period, a holiday over Christmas, where she is staying with her extended family. Given the local authority's overall case that it is only in respect of older children that significant concerns arise so as to require the removal of the children from the care of the parents, it is impossible, in my judgment, for the local authority to satisfy me that S is at risk of significant harm at Saint Kitts at present'*

As the above outlines and both cases demonstrate, the way cases are presented are important in terms of evidence and the risk. The local authority must carefully consider their position.

Notwithstanding the above, relief is upon to the local authority as each case is fact specific. The Supreme Court has affirmed that the inherent jurisdiction can be exercised with respect to a child who is a British national wherever s/he may be located (A v A and another (Children: Habitual Residence)[47].

In circumstances where a parent has already abducted a child out of England and Wales, the Local Authority can apply for orders under the inherent jurisdiction for a return to a non-Hague state (in England) or if the abduction has taken place to a country which is a signatory to the

---

47 (Reunite International Child Abduction Centre Intervening) [2013] UKSC 60, paragraph 60

1980 Hague Convention then the local authority can obtain declarations of habitual residence and other helpful provisions in the High Court to enable an application to be made through the Central Authority for the purposes of a 1980 Hague Convention case.

Further, Sir James Munby declared in Re M (Wardship)[48] outlined that the Crown's duty in relation to children extended, in the case of a child who was a British subject, to protect the child wherever he may be. The inherent jurisdiction was invoked to make orders with respect to children who had purportedly been taken by their parents to Syria in circumstances where it was feared their lives were at risk. He stated:

> '[32] …*I add that the use of the jurisdiction in cases where the risk to a child is of harm of the type that would engage Arts 2 or 3 of the European Convention for the Protection of Human Rights and Fundamental Freedoms 1950 (European Convention) – risk to life or risk of degrading or other inhuman treatment – is surely unproblematic. So wardship is surely an appropriate remedy, even if the child has already left the jurisdiction, in cases where the fear is that a child has been taken abroad for the purposes of forced marriage (as in Re KR and Re B) or so that she can be subject to female genital mutilation or (as here) where the fear is that a child has been taken abroad to travel to a dangerous war zone….*'

In circumstances where there are no existing proceedings but the local authority has reason to be concerned in respect of information they have, they can still apply to the inherent jurisdiction for necessary orders in order to safeguard the children. They will need to satisfy with the court why leave is needed. Any application must be supported by evidence in the form of a witness statement from the local authority.

Another point to emphasise in the context of public law proceedings and the inherent jurisdiction, the local authority can also apply for orders

48 [2015] EWHC 1433 (Fam), paragraph 30

such as Tipstaff orders. An example of this is in the case of City Council v A Mother & A Father & Ors (Care Proceedings Radicalisation)[49]. This was a case heard by Knowles J, who was concerned with four children in the context of public law proceedings. The issue was that of radicalisation. As paragraph 12 stated, the date in which an interim care order was made the judge:

> *'Alongside that order, the family's passports were surrendered to the Tipstaff, port alerts put in place, and orders made under the inherent jurisdiction, forbidding the removal of the younger children from the jurisdiction'*

Further, when proceedings were concluded in the case, Knowles J considered exercising the inherent jurisdiction in respect of prohibitions relating to travel. Her ladyship summarised the statutory provisions and the interplay with the inherent jurisdiction at paragraph 42, which stated:

> *'I have also been invited by the parties to make an order under the inherent jurisdiction, providing that Q's passport be held by the Local Authority until she is 18 years old. Such an order will prevent her travelling abroad before she is 18, unless she accompanies her family on a trip abroad, sanctioned by the Local Authority, or this court returns her passport to her. Given the concerns which have arisen in this case relating to travel abroad, and pursuant to Section 100(4) and Section 100(5) of the Children Act, such an order is, in my view, necessary, since without it there is reasonable cause to believe Q is likely to suffer significant harm. I am further satisfied that I should give the Local Authority permission to make its application for such an order, as the result which the Local Authority wishes to achieve could not be achieved through the making of an order either made out with the court's inherent jurisdiction, or for which the Local Authority is entitled to apply'*

[49] [2019] EWHC 3076 (Fam)

Forced Marriage Protection Orders and Female Genital Mutilation Orders

Over the last few years there have been a number of reported cases dealing with Female Genital Mutilation ['FGM'] and Forced Marriage Protection Orders ['FMPO'] which are often heard by High Court judges or Section 9 Judges. These types of proceedings can be urgent in nature where a party has information about the risk and then must make an application to the High Court. For example, if the authorities are provided with the information through the police, then a referral will be made to the local authority who will need to apply to the court.

A useful example of the inherent jurisdiction being invoked on a without notice basis where there was a risk of FGM and FMPO appears in a case heard by Knowles J in A Local Authority v X and Others[50]. At paragraphs 20 onwards, her ladyship considered on the basis of the evidence submitted:

> *'I am thus satisfied that both M and K require the protection of the court and that the appropriate means of protecting them is to make them wards of court alongside making forced marriage and female genital mutilation protection orders. I consider it almost inevitable that their welfare will require their return to this jurisdiction where the local authority can put in place arrangements for their care and protection.*
>
> *21. I am also satisfied that the exercise by the court of its inherent jurisdiction based on the girls' nationality does not risk creating a conflict of jurisdiction since Somaliland or Somalia itself are not signatories to any applicable treaty alongside/with the United Kingdom. Furthermore, it is unlikely that the courts in Somaliland or Somalia would entertain an application by a local authority for*

[50] [2019] EWHC 846 (Fam)

protective orders in respect of M and K which required their removal from both their mother's care and from that territory.

Finally, it is possible that there are steps which an English court may be able to take which might persuade the mother to obey the court's orders. In that regard, I note that the mother still claims child benefit for both M and K. The Forced Marriage Unit has raised the possibility that, as leverage to persuade the mother to comply with this court's orders, the payment of this benefit might in due course be suspended.

22. Likewise, I am satisfied that there is persuasive evidence that supports the making of forced marriage protection orders and female genital mutilation protection orders. The experiences of M and K's older siblings underscore the very high risk that the girls will become victims of forced marriage and female genital mutilation'

Turning to the issue of the inherent jurisdiction, her ladyship stated at paragraph 23:

'Finally, I observe that my orders pursuant to the inherent jurisdiction and to the relevant statutes are purely protective in nature. They do not seek to prescribe matters concerning the care of the girls, contact with them or their education or medical treatment'.

In respect of both FGM and FMPO it must be outlined that historically they were dealt with in the High Court through the inherent jurisdiction. Now statute exists, namely Family Law Act 1996 (part 4) or the Female Genital Mutilation Act 2003, Schedule 2 in the specified courts in accordance with the procedure set out in FPR 2010, r 11. The High Court's inherent jurisdiction may however still be invoked where the provisions of the Act do not cover the circumstances of the individual case. Further, where there is the risk of FGM or FMPO these proceedings are often heard in parallel to public law proceedings and a number of other additional orders can be made in the High Court utilising the inherent jurisdiction.

For completeness, the provisions of the FMPO are wide ranging and Section 63 of the FLA specifies:

'(1) The court may make an order for the purposes of protecting—

(a) a person from being forced into a marriage or from any attempt to be forced into a marriage; or

(b) a person who has been forced into a marriage.

(2) In deciding whether to exercise its powers under this section and, if so, in what manner, the court must have regard to all the circumstances including the need to secure the health, safety and well-being of the person to be protected'

In terms of the contents of such an order:

'Contents of orders

(1) A forced marriage protection order may contain—

(a) such prohibitions, restrictions or requirements; and

(b) such other terms;

as the court considers appropriate for the purposes of the order.

(2) The terms of such orders may, in particular, relate to—

(a) conduct outside England and Wales as well as (or instead of) conduct within England and Wales;

(b) respondents who are, or may become, involved in other respects as well as (or instead of) respondents who force or attempt to force, or may force or attempt to force, a person to enter into a marriage;

(c) other persons who are, or may become, involved in other respects as well as respondents of any kind.

(3) For the purposes of subsection (2) examples of involvement in other respects are—

(a) aiding, abetting, counselling, procuring, encouraging or assisting another person to force, or to attempt to force, a person to enter into a marriage; or

(b) conspiring to force, or to attempt to force, a person to enter into a marriage.'

Section 63C outlines that such orders can be made without notice or on notice.

In terms of FGM:

In Fornah v Secretary of State for the Home Department[51] Baroness Hale observed the following in respect of FGM [paragraph 94]:

'... the procedure will almost inevitably amount to either torture or to other cruel, inhuman or degrading treatment within the meaning, not only of article 3 of the European Convention on Human Rights, but also of article 1 or 16 of the Convention against Torture and other Cruel, Inhuman or Degrading Treatment or Punishment, article 7 of the International Covenant on Civil and Political Rights, and article 37(a) of the Convention on the Rights of the Child.'

The powers are wide-ranging. Cobb J in Re X (Female Genital Mutilation Protection Order No.2)[52] having considered the Court of

[51] [2006] UKHL 46, paragraph 94

[52] [2019] EWHC 1990

Appeal in Re X (A Child)(FGMPO distilled the key principles at paragraph 6:

> *'i) There is no dispute that FGM is a barbaric and criminal act; this point needs no amplification but may benefit from repetition. Although the World Health Organisation categorise FGM into four main types (each describing the specific cutting performed, summarised as I. Clitoridectomy, II. Excision, III. Infibulation and IV. Other), it is important that no one type of FGM should be regarded as less objectionable or heinous than another (see [14]-[16] and [52] below). FGM in whatever form is torturous within the context of Article 3 ECHR, and is "cruel, discriminatory and degrading" (see [27] below);*
>
> *ii) In this situation, and in many like it, the rights to respect for private and family life (Article 8 ECHR) and the right to protection from torture (Article 3) are engaged; any interference with the Article 8 rights has to be necessary and proportionate, having regard to the harm to be protected against (see [27]-[29] below);*
>
> *iii) In a re-hearing involving a factual dispute, the trial judge invariably faces the special difficulty of assessing evidence which has been previously rehearsed, tested and critiqued. This is a particular challenge in a case, such as this, when the case for the applicant Local Authority turns largely on what the protagonists have previously said, or are reported to have said, or apparently believed, and/or say now about the key issues (see [31]-[32] below);*
>
> *iv) When considering whether (and if so to what extent) to impose orders under Schedule 2 of the 2003 Act to support a FGMPO, it is helpful to assess the risks to the child by reference to the contextual 'macro' factors which are relevant to the likelihood of genital cutting (i.e. the prevalence of FGM in the country, the societal expectation of FGM, the effectiveness of local law enforcement agencies etc.) together with the associated safeguards, and the individual 'micro' factors and safeguards pertaining to the particular case and to the subject child(ren) and family (see [91] below);*

v) Risk assessment in this context, as in other contexts in family law, should be an ongoing process. Risk is generally dynamic, not static; the barometer of risk is often relatively sensitive. Courts should be alert to the possibility that as or when new evidence emerges, and/or the contextual or individual characteristics of a given situation shift, so the index of risk may well shift (see [106] below)'

In terms of the law, Cobb J went further at paragraph 20 in considering the statutory provisions. In particular, the circumstances of a local authority involvement and their status as a party. Helpfully, his lordship reminded all the following: '*The 2003 Act* specifically preserves the right for the court to use any of its other powers to protect a girl in these circumstances, including the inherent jurisdiction (*Schedule 2, para.16*)'. For context, the summary of the law was at paragraph 20:

20. *'Section 5A and Schedule 2 (Part 1) of the 2003 Act contain the legislative powers for the civil injunctive order under consideration in this case. Such orders are made (Schedule 2 para.1(1)) "for the purposes of – (a) protecting a girl against the commission of a genital mutilation offence". Schedule 2 para.1(2) materially provides that:*

"In deciding whether to exercise its powers under this paragraph and, if so, in what manner, the court must have regard to all the circumstances, including the need to secure the health, safety and well-being of the girl to be protected."

Schedule 2 para.1(3) provides that an order may contain:

"(a) such prohibitions, restrictions or requirements, and (b) such other terms, as the court considers appropriate for the purposes of the order."

The terms of the order may extend to conduct outside of England and Wales (as well as (or instead of) conduct within England and Wales) (see para.1(4) Schedule 2, of the 2003 Act). The 2003

Act specifically preserves the right for the court to use any of its other powers to protect a girl in these circumstances, including the inherent jurisdiction (Schedule 2, para.16).

21. *There is no fixed period of time for which a court can make the order (see para.1(6) schedule 2 of the 2003 Act).*

22. *The Local Authority is a relevant 'third party' under the Schedule 2, para.2(2)(b)/(7) of the 2003 Act and is therefore entitled to bring this application.*

23. *The burden of proving the facts relevant to support the application lies squarely on the Local Authority. Where I make findings within the narrative below, I do so by reference to the ordinary civil standard of proof, and having specific regard to the comments of Lord Hoffman in Re B (Care Proceedings: Standard of Proof) [2008] UKHL 35 at para [2][4]. The Local Authority must also demonstrate both the necessity and the proportionality of the range of protective orders sought in this case, specifically the worldwide travel ban. It is not for the parents to prove that X is not at risk of FGM, nor is it for them to prove that it is safe for X to travel, nor that any risk can be mitigated.*

24. *A useful starting point for my review of the law is the judgment of the Court of Appeal in the instant case ([2018] EWCA Civ 1825 at [23]-[34]). I do not intend to reproduce those paragraphs here. The statutory discretion afforded to the court when considering whether to make an order (see [20] above) is widely drawn. Moylan LJ observed that the "very broad" powers in Schedule 2 para.1(2) of the 2003 Act provide no real guidance "as to the approach the court should take when determining whether and, if so, in what manner to exercise its powers" ([2018] EWCA Civ 1825 at [24]).*

25. *Breach of the civil injunctive order ("[a] person who without reasonable excuse does anything that the person is prohibited from*

doing by an FGM protection order") is punishable as an offence (Schedule 2, para.4) and the guilty party faces a maximum of 5 years custody if tried on indictment. Much wider sentencing powers are available for those prosecuted for an offence under Sections 1, 2 or 3 of the 2003 Act.

26. *On 15 March 2019, during the course of this hearing, the Children Act 1989 (Amendment) (Female Genital Mutilation) Act 2019 came into force; this has the effect of including civil/family proceedings for a FGMPO within the definition of 'family proceedings' in section 8(4) CA 1989. It enables care proceedings to be brought within the same application as an application for a FGMPO. Care proceedings have not been seriously contemplated in the instant case.*

27. *The practice of FGM is "an abuse of human rights" (see Re B and G (Children)(No 2) [2015] 1 FLR 905 at [55]); it is well-recognised that FGM violates Article 3 of the ECHR, which serves to protect persons from "torture or ... inhuman or degrading treatment or punishment". As Baroness Hale observed in Fornah v Secretary of State for the Home Department [2006] UKHL 46; [2007] 1 AC 412, at [94]:*

"... the procedure will almost inevitably amount either to torture or to other cruel, inhuman or degrading treatment within the meaning, not only of article 3 of the European Convention on Human Rights, but also of article 1 or 16 of the Convention against Torture and other Cruel, Inhuman or Degrading Treatment or Punishment, article 7 of the International Covenant on Civil and Political Rights, and article 37(a) of the Convention on the Rights of the Child".

And Lord Bingham in the same case said this at [8]:

"FGM has been condemned as cruel, discriminatory and degrading by a long series of international instruments, declarations,

resolutions, pronouncements and recommendations. … Therefore those cultural practices that involve "severe pain and suffering" for the woman or the girl child, those that do not respect the physical integrity of the female body, must receive maximum international scrutiny and agitation. It is imperative that practices such as female genital mutilation, honour killings, Sati or any other form of cultural practice that brutalizes the female body receive international attention, and international leverage should be used to ensure that these practices are curtailed and eliminated as quickly as possible".

28. *When confronted with a case of suspected or threatened FGM, the court has an obligation "to take measures within the scope of [the court's] powers which, judged reasonably, might have been expected to avoid the risk" of FGM where that risk is "real and immediate" (see by analogy Osman v United Kingdom (1998) 29 EHRR 245, and E v Chief Constable of the Royal Ulster Constabulary and another [2009] 1 AC 536). In E v United Kingdom (2003) 36 EHRR 519 it was said that:*

"A failure to take reasonably available measures which could have had a real prospect of altering the outcome or mitigating the harm is sufficient to engage the responsibility of the state" (para.99).

29. *In this case, as in many like it, Article 8 ECHR is actively engaged as X and her parents have a right (albeit qualified) to respect for their family life. In balancing the Article 3 and Article 8 rights of X, I must be careful to ensure that "the interference with [X's] Article 8 rights, and those of her … family… [are]… limited to that which is necessary to protect her Article 3 rights" per Hayden J in A Local Authority v M & N [2018] EWHC 870 (Fam), [2018] 4 WLR 98. endorsed by Moylan LJ in his judgment in this case at [30]'.*

The statutory provisions are therefore wide-ranging and powerful and practitioners involved in such proceedings should remind themselves of the words of Cobb J as the judgment provides an authoritative analysis on the relevant issues.

Deprivation of Liberty

This is an area of law that has attracted much attention over the last few years. Helpfully, the Supreme Court considered the issue in 2021 in the matter of Re T. Lady Black focused on Section 100 of the Children Act 1989 at paragraphs 118 and 119 of the judgment:

'Having started with prohibiting the use of the inherent jurisdiction to place the child in local authority care or under their supervision, it then prevents the court using the inherent jurisdiction to order the accommodation of a child by a local authority, and, of course, prevents it being used to put the local authority in a position to determine any question in connection with parental responsibility. This seems to me to be entirely consistent with the aim being to confine matters to the statutory scheme in Part IV of the Children Act 1989, the thinking being that a local authority needing the power to determine any question in connection with parental responsibility must seek it through the medium of a care order.

'It must also be borne in mind that Parliament made it very clear that it was not intended that the inherent jurisdiction should be entirely unavailable to local authorities, and that it appreciated that there could be cases in which it would be necessary to have recourse to it because there was reason to believe that the child would otherwise be likely to suffer significant harm. *This is evident from sections 100(3) to (5). Like the express prohibitions in sections 100(1) and (2), the more general conditions imposed by subsections (3) to (5) are shaped to confine the local authority to orders otherwise available to them but building in a safety net where those other orders would not achieve the required result in a risky situation.' [emphasis added'*

In terms of the local authority invoking the inherent jurisdiction in the context of deprivation of liberty but also in the wider sense, the Supreme Court at paragraph 119 outlined:

> '119. *It must also be borne in mind that Parliament made it very clear that it was not intended that the inherent jurisdiction should be entirely unavailable to local authorities, and that it appreciated that there could be cases in which it would be necessary to have recourse to it because there was reason to believe that the child would otherwise be likely to suffer significant harm. This is evident from sections 100(3) to (5). Like the express prohibitions in sections 100(1) and (2), the more general conditions imposed by subsections (3) to (5) are shaped to confine the local authority to orders otherwise available to them, but building in a safety net where those other orders would not achieve the required result in a risky situation.*
>
> 120. *Turning to the requirement in section 100(4)(a) that leave may only be granted if the desired result could not be achieved through another form of order, this is satisfied, it seems to me. Mostyn J was not satisfied that T's consent was authentic and likely to endure so this is not a case in which to consider the impact of more robust consent of a Gillick-competent 15-year-old child. The court's authorisation was undoubtedly required in this case for any deprivation of her liberty. An application under section 25 could not be made because no approved "secure accommodation" was available for T (as to which I will say more later), and there was no means by which the local authority could seek the authorisation it required other than under the inherent jurisdiction. As for section 100(4)(b) (likely significant harm), it has not been argued that it was unnecessary for T to be in the placements provided by the local authority, her argument being simply that there was no need for a court order because reliance could be placed on her consent. I will look briefly, later, at the impact of consent more generally but, as I have said, the facts here did not provide any foundation for this particular argument.*

> *121. Accordingly, I do not consider that the express terms of section 100 were an obstacle to the local authority's application under the inherent jurisdiction'.*

However, before embarking upon the inherent jurisdiction and the deprivation of liberty, the reason why the inherent jurisdiction is invoked in such proceedings must briefly be touched upon as the issue arises from the provisions relating to secure accommodation.

Secure Accommodation

There is a statutory basis regulating the use of secure accommodation in respect of children. Section 25 of the Children Act 1989 states:

> *'25. Use of accommodation for restricting liberty*
>
> *(1) Subject to the following provisions of this section, a child who is being looked after by a local authority in England or Wales may not be placed, and, if placed, may not be kept, in accommodation in England or Scotland provided for the purpose of restricting liberty ("secure accommodation") unless it appears*
>
> *(a) that: -*
>
> *(i) he has a history of absconding and is likely to abscond from any other description of accommodation; and*
>
> *(ii) if he absconds, he is likely to suffer significant harm; or*
>
> *(b) that if he is kept in any other description of accommodation he is likely to injure himself or other persons.'*

In Re B (Secure Accommodation)[53] Baker LJ considered the provisions and having regard to welfare and proportionality distilled the following:

> *'i) Is the subject child being "looked after" by a local authority, or, alternatively, does he or she fall within one of the other categories specified in regulation 7 of the Children (Secure Accommodation) Regulations 1991?*
>
> *ii) Is the accommodation where the local authority proposes to place the child "secure accommodation", i.e. is it designed for or have as its primary purpose the restriction of liberty?*
>
> *iii) Is the court satisfied (a) that (i) the child has a history of absconding and is likely to abscond from any other description of accommodation, and (ii) if he/she absconds, he/she is likely to suffer significant harm or (b) that if kept in any other description of accommodation, he/she is likely to injure himself or other persons?*
>
> *iv) If the local authority is proposing to place the child in a secure children's home in England, has the accommodation been approved by the Secretary of State for use as secure accommodation? If the local authority is proposing to place the child in a children's home in Scotland, is the accommodation provided by a service which has been approved by the Scottish Ministers?*
>
> *v) Does the proposed order safeguard and promote the child's welfare?*
>
> *vi) Is the order proportionate, i.e. do the benefits of the proposed placement outweigh the infringement of rights?'*

53 [2019] EWCA Civ 2025, paragraph 98

Further, in respect of secure accommodation, Hayden J in London Borough of Barking and Dagenham v SS[54] summarised the provisions and the impact of them:

> '*It scarcely needs to be said that restricting the liberty of a child is an extremely serious step, especially where the child has not committed any criminal offence, nor is alleged to have committed any criminal offence. It is for this reason that the process is tightly regulated by the Children Act 1989 in the way I have set out, but also in the Children (Secure Accommodation) Regulations 1991 and the Children (Secure Accommodation No.2) Regulations 1991.*'

Accordingly, if there is a statutory provision, why the need to consider deprivation of liberty? As MacDonald J stated in Lancashire County Council v G and N[55]

> '*By reason of an increasing shortage of secure placements approved as such by the Secretary of State and, Mr Jones submits, an increasing reluctance on the part of those secure placements to accept children with the level and complexity of needs demonstrated by children like G, the courts have increasingly been asked to sanction the placement of children in G's position in regulated, and even unregulated placements under the auspices of an order made under the inherent jurisdiction of the High Court authorising the deprivation of their liberty as an alternative to secure accommodation authorised under s 25 of the Children Act 1989*'

The National Deprivation of Liberty Court

On 4th July 2022, the President of the Family Division announced the launch of the National Deprivation of Liberty Court (DoLs). This court is based in the Royal Courts of Justice and was created to deal with

---

54 [2014] EWHC 4436 (Fam), paragraph 15

55 [2020] EWHC 2828 (Fam), paragraph 31

applications seeking authorisation to deprive children of their liberty. The Court is supported by two family High Court Judge / Deputy High Court judges each week with a dedicated administrative team.

Those working in the public law field of family law will be aware of the numerous reported cases from the high courts about the lack of sufficient provision for children. For example, in Lancashire County Council v G and N[56] MacDonald J outlined the stark facts of his case and the difficulties at paragraphs 7 and 8 as follows:

> *'In the foregoing circumstances G, a vulnerable young woman with multifaceted difficulties and at high risk of serious self-harm or suicide who remains inappropriately placed on an adult mental health ward will, if discharged from her current detention under s.2 of the Mental Health Act 1983 at some point today, have nowhere to go unless the court authorises the deprivation of her liberty at an unregistered placement that has stated its intention not to seek registration and which the Children's Guardian does not feel able to endorse as being in her best interests.*
>
> *The stark choice thus faced by the court is to refuse to authorise the deprivation of G's liberty in an unregistered placement, which will result in her discharge into the community where she will almost certainly cause herself possibly fatal harm, or to authorise the deprivation of G's liberty in an unregistered placement that all parties agree is sub-optimal from the perspective of her welfare because that unregulated placement is, quite simply, the only option available'*

Baker LJ in Re B (Secure Accommodation)[57] went on to describe how and why the inherent jurisdiction comes into play, commenting at 102:

---

56 [2020] EWHC 2828 (Fam)

57 [2019] EWCA Civ 2025

'*Where, however, the local authority applies under s.25 and all the relevant criteria for keeping a child in 'secure accommodation' under the section are satisfied, the court is required, by s.25(4), to make an order under that section authorising the child to be kept in such accommodation. To exercise the inherent jurisdiction in such circumstances would cut across the statutory scheme*'

The Inherent jurisdiction and deprivation of liberty – the test

Given the significant issues raised in deprivation of liberty cases, it is important practitioners are aware of the requirements and procedures that must be met. This is particularly important for a local authority who is making the application. Cobb J reviewed the existing case law in Re RD (Deprivation or Restriction of Liberty)[58] and summarised the position as follows:

'*i) 'Free to leave' does not mean leaving for the purpose of some trip or outing approved by those managing the institution; it means leaving in the sense of removing herself permanently in order to live where and with whom she chooses (Re A-F [2018] EWHC 138 (Fam) at [14], repeating comments made in JE v DE at [115], which had been cited with approval in Re D (A Child) [2017] EWCA Civ 1695, [22]);*

ii) It is accepted wisdom that a typical fourteen or fifteen-year old is not free to leave her home (Re A-F at [31](i));

iii) The terms 'complete' or 'constant' define 'supervision' and 'control' as indicating something like 'total', 'unremitting', 'thorough', and/or 'unqualified' (Re RD (Deprivation or Restriction of Liberty) at [31]);

iv) It does not matter whether the object is to protect, treat or care in some way for the person taken into confinement (Cheshire West and Chester v P at [28]);

58 [2018] EWFC 47

v) The comparative benevolence of living arrangements should not blind the court to their essential character if indeed those arrangements constitute a deprivation of liberty (Cheshire West and Chester v P at [35]);

vi) What it means to be deprived of liberty must be the same for everyone, whether or not they have physical or mental disabilities (Cheshire West and Chester v P at [46]);

vii) The person's compliance or lack of objection, the relative normality of the placement (whatever the comparison made) and the reason or purpose behind a particular placement are not relevant factors (Cheshire West and Chester v P at [50]);

viii) The distinction between deprivation and restriction is a matter of "degree or intensity" and "in the end, it is the constraints that matter" (Cheshire West and Chester v P at [56]);

ix) The question whether a child is restricted as a matter of fact is to be determined by comparing the extent of the child's actual freedom with someone of the child's age and station whose freedom is not limited (Cheshire West and Chester v P at [77]);

x) The sensible and humane comparison to be drawn is that between the situation of the child with the ordinary lives which young people of their ages might live at home with their families (Cheshire West and Chester v P at [47]);

xi) The 'acid test' has to be directly applied on each case to the circumstances of the individual under review. Where that individual is a child or young person, particular considerations apply (Re A-F at [30])'

In terms of procedural steps to undertake, MacDonald J had regard to the case law and Cobb J's decision above and summarised the steps in Lancashire County Council v G and N[59]:

> *'The guidance requires the following steps to be taken when an application is made to the court for an order under the court's inherent jurisdiction to authorise the deprivation of the liberty of a child:*
>
> *i) The applicant should make the court explicitly aware of the registration status of those providing or seeking to provide the care and accommodation for the child.*
>
> *ii) If those providing, carrying on and managing the service are not registered, this must be made clear to the court. The court should be made aware of the reasons why registration is not required or the reasons for the delay in seeking registration.*
>
> *iii) The applicant must make the court aware of the steps it is taking (in the absence of the provision falling within Ofsted or CIW's scope of registration) to ensure that the premises and support being provided are safe and suitable for the child accommodated.*
>
> *iv) Due to the vulnerability of the children likely to be subject to an order authorising a deprivation of their liberty, when a child is to be provided with care and accommodation in an unregistered children's home or unregistered care home service, the court will need to be satisfied that steps are being taken to apply for the necessary registration.*
>
> *v) The court should also be informed by the local authority of the steps the local authority is taking in the meantime to assure itself that the premises, those working at the premises and the care being given are safe and suitable for the accommodated child.*

59 [2020] EWHC 2828 (Fam), paragraph 48

vi) Where an application for registration has been submitted to Ofsted or CIW, the court should be made aware of the exact status of that application.

vii) If an order is granted and no application for registration has been made, then the court order should provide that the application for registration should be submitted to Ofsted or CIW within 7 working days from the date of the order.

viii) Once the court is satisfied that a complete application has been received by Ofsted or CIW, the court will review the situation regarding the registration status of those carrying on and managing the children's home or care home service in a further 12 weeks. Such review (which may be on paper) will be in addition to any review the court requires to ascertain whether the deprivation of liberty should continue.

ix) If the court has not received confirmation from the local authority within 10 working days of the initial order that a complete application for registration has been received by Ofsted or CIW, the court should list the matter for a further immediate hearing.

x) If registration is refused or the applications for registration are withdrawn, the local authority should advise the court of this as a matter of urgency. The court will take this into account when deciding whether the placement of the child in the unregistered children's home or unregistered care home service continues to be in the child's best interests'

The case of Re CC (A Child)[60] is a useful case to illustrate where a deprivation of liberty order through the inherent jurisdiction was not granted. The case is a 2023 authority where each party was contesting

---

60 [2023] EWHC 2179 (Fam)

the local authority case. As paragraph 1 outlines in terms of the factual matrix:

> *'A London Borough ("the Local Authority") applies under the inherent jurisdiction of the High Court for authorisation of arrangements made by the Local Authority which have resulted in CC being deprived of her liberty whilst she is residing at an Ofsted registered children's home located in a rural area some distance out of London ("the Placement"). This application is actively opposed by both CC's Mother and her Guardian. Both submit that there is no justification for depriving CC of her liberty whilst she is placed in the Placement and that the only reason that the Local Authority is seeking this order is the concern that, absent an order, the Placement may give notice to terminate the Placement. The position of the Guardian is that, as a matter of principle, absent good evidence based on the risks to a young person, a threat by a private provider to terminate a placement should be insufficient to justify the court making a deprivation of liberty order'*

The local authority sought the following restrictions:

> *'i) CC should be supervised by staff from the Placement at all times, with staff following her and keeping her in their line of sight should CC decide to leave the Placement without permission, or without staff. In the event CC were to leave without supervision or permission, efforts would be made to encourage her to return to the Placement and to support her on a one-to-one basis. In the event this is unsuccessful, police and the local authority would be notified;*
>
> *ii) When leaving the Placement for planned activities, CC will always be accompanied by a member of staff;*
>
> *iii) The doors to the Placement are to remain locked to CC at all times. CCTV is used in connection with the accommodation and contributes towards the ongoing supervision of those who are living at the Placement;*

iv) CC is not to have access to the internet on any devices; and

v) Trained staff at the Placement are entitled, as a last resort, to use reasonable force to prevent CC self-harming or harming others'

Upon considering the evidence and the law on the use of deprivation of liberty and inherent jurisdiction, the application was refused. His lordship stated at paragraph 59 and 60 of the case:

'In this case, on the evidence before me at present, I have to reach the conclusion that the test in paragraph 141 of Re T is not met. The Local Authority have never, as far as I am aware, explored the option of section 25 accommodation for CC, even if the Local Authority were to have reached the view that she met the section 25 statutory criteria, which appears to me to be doubtful. Instead, they have identified what they felt was appropriate residential accommodation, namely the Placement, and having decided to place CC there, find themselves having to grapple with the difficulty that Cambian has said it was not prepared to continue the Placement unless the Local Authority sought and obtained a DOLS order allowing the provider to deprive CC of her liberty between Monday and Friday.

In those circumstances it seems to me to impermissible to authorise the deprivation of liberty under the inherent jurisdiction for the reason identified by Lady Black in the above passage, namely that to do so would cut unacceptably across the statutory scheme which is intended to operate to govern which categories of children can be placed in secure accommodation. It is one thing for a DOL order to be made for a child who satisfies the section 25 CA criteria but for whom no secure accommodation can be found. It is wholly different to make a DOL order for a child that does not satisfy the criteria and where no section 25 accommodation has ever been looked for. I accept that the only way that the Local Authority can lawfully make arrangements which deprive CC of her liberty is for the Court to make a DOL order exercising the inherent jurisdiction, but as Lady Black acknowledges, that power should only be used if exercising the power does not cut across the statutory scheme under section 25 CA, and it plainly does here'.

Therefore, whilst there is now a specialist court in respect of deprivation of liberty proceedings to ensure cases can be heard by a specialist judge, there is also a vast amount of case law on the issue. The cases need to be properly presented by the applicant, who would be the local authority.

Declarations

There can be many circumstances where the local authority may wish to make an application pursuant to the inherent jurisdiction of the High Court in order to obtain a declaration. For example, a declaration that their action as a local authority is lawful.

A useful example is the authority of A Local Authority v Y & Anor (Notification of The Father and Relatives)[61]. This case was heard by Theis J and her ladyship was concerned with and application by the local authority seeking a declaration that they are not required to undertake any further steps to notify the maternal and paternal family regarding X, a child now age 5 months. X's father and the paternal family are unaware of X's birth. This was a case of complexity, but her ladyship reviewed the Court of Appeal authorities and the statutory provisions. In coming to a conclusion and making the declaration, the reasons for doing as appears in the judgment at paragraph 46:

'(1) The court recognises the significant breach of an individual's Article 8 right to family and private life not to be informed of the existence of their child or a child they are related to. This is particularly so regarding the father in this case, but also extends to the members of the wider family who this application relates.

61 [2023] EWHC 2040 (Fam)

(2) This equally applies in relation to the child concerned who has a right to know their parent and wider birth family members.

(3) However, these two important considerations need to be balanced with the particular circumstances of the child, X, who is the focus of the application to withhold notice about.

(4) In this case the father does not hold parental responsibility for X and the evidence demonstrates that the father does not exercise the parental responsibility he has relating to his older two children in the mother's care, other than attending for contact on a sporadic basis when they spend time with his mother.

(5) Neither the father nor the wider family currently exercise any Article 8 rights in relation to X.

(6) The evidence demonstrates that the father's involvement with his older children has been sporadic and unreliable. He accepted he was unable to care for child B and has had no contact with him since his placement for adoption. In relation to the two children in the mother's care the father's contact has been erratic.

(7) Bearing in mind the background and the father's particular difficulties with his history of abusive behaviour, his mental health and emotional dysregulation he is very unlikely to be able to care for X or have consistent and reliable continuing contact with him.

(8) The same applies regarding the wider paternal and maternal family bearing in mind the history and the evidence the court has seen regarding their particular circumstances and their involvement with the older children.

(9) Whilst it is right the father has an established relationship with X's mother, that relationship has featured abusive behaviour by the father towards the mother such that the police have been involved on repeated occasions, he has been subject to police bail which the mother alleges he

has breached and the court has made a non-molestation order against the father based on the corroborated evidence provided by the mother. There is a real risk, in my judgment, that if he is notified either directly or indirectly his behaviour is likely to increase the risk of harm to the mother and the children she cares for based on the evidence from the mother, corroborated by the evidence from the police and the local authority regarding the father's behaviour towards the mother during their relationship, his previous partners and his own mother. It is also an important feature of this case that due to the history it is unlikely that any measures put in place will mitigate the level of risk of harm to the mother and the children who live with her resulting from the father's behaviour.

(10) The evidence the court has about the mother, supported by the assessments of the local authority and Children's Guardian, is that her decision was reached with X's interests being her primary focus. The evidence she relies upon regarding the father's behaviour is supported by third-party material and covers an extended period of time.

(11) There is a real risk that notification to the father and/or the wider family will cause considerable delay in decisions being made for X in circumstances where there has already been delay and the evidence demonstrates limited benefit to X in terms of future care within the family. The risks of and incidental to notification are outweighed by any benefits for X. The local authority and the mother are committed to life story work for X, so he will have that important information available to him. Whilst it is recognised that this order will impact on X's ability to be able to have any relationship with his older siblings in the care of the mother, the local authority are actively looking at the option of him being placed with either of his half siblings who are currently in separate adoptive placements. Any further delay may risk that option being considered.

(12) I accept the evidence of the Children's Guardian, who has undertaken her own careful assessment of the mother and then considered it against the objective third party safeguarding

information. Her reasoned and realistic analysis of the placement options for X within the family, the risks to the mother and the children she cares for if notification is given and the impact on X of the inevitable delay if the application was not granted is compelling. It is a careful and well-reasoned analysis that provides a secure foundation for reaching the conclusion I have in this case'

The above demonstrates the complex factors in play in respect of the law but also the issues in respect of risk and the child's welfare. As a consequence of the law, the local authority had no choice in order to fulfil their duties to apply to the Court for a declaration and this serves as a useful example of the ability of the local authority to seek such relief in these types of scenarios.

Ensuring the right application is made

The local authority must take care about what relief they seek under the inherent jurisdiction, regardless of the particular issues in the case. The recent case of Re S[62] serves as a useful reminder in a case heard by the President of the Family Division. The originating application was that the local authority applied for leave to invoke the inherent jurisdiction of the High Court in order to prevent a young person who was then aged 15 years, from travelling to Country X in order to undergo surgery, namely a double mastectomy.

At paragraph 12 and 13, his lordship when reviewing the case chronology and litigation stated the following, in respect of a Section 37 report and the inherent jurisdiction:

'12. The description of the local authority position in the s 37 report is striking. CA 1989, s 100(4)(a) makes plain that access to the inherent jurisdiction is only available if the result that the local authority wishes to achieve cannot be gained by applying for an order that the authority

62 (inherent jurisdiction: transgender surgery abroad) [2023] EWHC 347 (Fam)

> *is otherwise entitled to apply for under the statutory scheme. This is a basic tenet of the CA 1989 and should be well known to all lawyers who practice in this field. When measured against s 100(4), the s 37 report is legally incoherent by, firstly, contemplating that the local authority could apply for a care order but, for the time being, has decided not to do so, and, secondly, by relying upon the existing inherent jurisdiction order as obviating the need to apply for a care order. The latter point distorts the legal structure by turning it through 180 degrees. If the remedy that a local authority seeks can be obtained by application for a order that is entitled to apply for then, by virtue of s 100(4)+(5), that is the procedural course that it must follow and the High Court will be barred from granting leave to apply for an order under the inherent jurisdiction. The fact, as this local authority has indicated, that the authority would prefer not to apply for a care order is of no relevance.*
>
> *13. Can I make it plain that, by criticising the legal approach described in the s 37 report, I do not seek to criticise its author, who was a newly qualified social worker. My criticism is of the corporation, rather than any individual. Here the authority was embarked upon an unusual legal intervention, supported by solicitors and counsel. The responsibility of ensuring that the basic legal building blocks upon which the application was based were legally sound was a corporate one, and there was a duty to ensure that this was correctly set out within the s 37 process'*

It is therefore clear, that his Lordship outlined very clearly a responsibility on practitioners to have regard to the relevant provisions and the appropriateness of embarking upon the inherent jurisdiction of the High Court.

Conclusion

This chapter outlines that the local authority can utilise the inherent jurisdiction through a variety of ways. The main area that it is used is that of the deprivation of liberty cases given the specialist court that is now in existence. However, there can be numerous fact-specific or even unique cases, where the inherent jurisdiction is required to be utilised. As a consequence of the local authority being the state, they have a number of resources available to them but also in respect of children, a significant number of duties to safeguard the most vulnerable in society. Therefore, when seeking relief, the appropriate procedures need to be embarked upon. A lot of the law can be found within case law and there are decades and decades of cases relating to the interpretation of the inherent jurisdiction in cases involving the local authority. With greater transparency, more judgments are being published. This can either assist parties in finding similar cases applying the principles or it can have a detrimental effect, in circumstances where the local authority may seek relief and it is not granted, but publicly known.

CHAPTER SIX

THE INHERENT JURISDICTION AND INJUNCTIVE ORDERS

Introduction

Separate to the prohibitive orders contained within Tipstaff orders, this chapter will consider the mechanism in which injunctions can be applied for using the inherent jurisdiction. This is interlinked between private law disputes between parents but also can appear in the context of public law involvement, for example in cases involving the local authority in fresh proceedings or existing public law proceedings.

The Local Authority and Injunctive Provisions

There might be scenarios in which the local authority may seek an injunction pursuant to the inherent jurisdiction of the High Court. For example, HHL Bellamy (sitting as a High Court Judge) in Re FD (Inherent Jurisdiction: Power of Arrest)[63] stated the following at paragraph 24:

> *'It is also now well-established that the essence of the court's inherent protective jurisdiction is to be flexible so as to be able to respond to social needs and changing social values.'*

The first step for a local authority (or in fact anyone when seeking to invoke the inherent jurisdiction) when applying for an injunctive order

---

63 [2016] EWHC 2358 (Fam)

is, whether it is capable of enforcement. In Re J (A Child)[64] [2013] EWHC 2694 (Fam) the President observed:

> *'61. On the other hand, and because equity does not act in vain, the court will not grant an injunction which is ineffectual or, to use the Latin, a mere brutum fulmen. As Kerr LJ put it in the passage from which I have already quoted, "our courts will not make orders which they cannot enforce."*
>
> *'62. What approach should the court adopt in coming to a decision as to how to exercise its discretion? This is a matter for another day, when there is fuller argument than was appropriate in the present case. Here I merely note that in Wookey Butler-Sloss LJ said that "there must be a real possibility that the order, if made, will be enforceable," while in Dadourian Group International Inc v Simms and others (Practice Note) [2006] EWCA Civ 399, [2006] 1 WLR 2499, para [35], Arden LJ said that "the court must be astute to see that there is a real prospect that something will be gained.'*

However, the case of G (Wardship) (Jurisdiction: Power of Arrest)[65] established that there was no power within proceedings under the inherent jurisdiction (whether in wardship or not) for the court to attach a power or arrest to an injunction in the absence of any statutory authority to do so.

Another consideration for a local authority is whether they are able to utilise the inherent jurisdiction to apply for a non-molestation order under the Family Law Act 1996. The provisions in respect of a power of arrest is governed by FLA 1996, s.42A(1) which was inserted by the Domestic Violence, Crime and Victims Act 2004 which states that "*a person who without reasonable excuse does anything that he is prohibited from doing by a non-molestation order is guilty of an offence*'. Consequently,

[64] [2013] EWHC 2694 (Fam)

[65] [1983] 4 FLR 538

a breach of a non-molestation order is therefore a matter of criminal law in relation to which the police may take action.

In order to first ascertain whether the inherent jurisdiction can come to the rescue for a local authority, the statutory provisions must be outlined.

Section 42 of the FLA deals with "non-molestation orders". By s.42(1) it is provided that:

> *'In this Part a "non-molestation order" means an order containing either or both of the following provisions:*
>
> *(a)...*
>
> *(b) provision prohibiting the respondent from molesting a relevant child.'*

The jurisdiction to make a non-molestation order is set out in s.42(2):

> *'The court may make a non-molestation order:*
>
> *(a) if an application for the order has been made (whether in other family proceedings or without any other family proceedings being instituted) by a person who is associated with the respondent; or*
>
> *(b) if in any family proceedings to which the respondent is a party the court considers that the order should be made for the benefit of any other party to the proceedings or any relevant child even though no such application has been made.'*

In terms of 'family proceedings' in FLA 1996, Part 4 is defined in s 63(1) as meaning proceedings 'under the inherent jurisdiction of the High Court in relation to children' or 'under the enactments mentioned in [s 63(2)]', which contains a comprehensive list of family proceedings.

FLA 1996 s.42A establishes the criminal offence of breaching a non-molestation order, with a punishment up to 5 years imprison.

FLA 1996, s.62(2) defines 'relevant child' as follows:

> *'In this Part "relevant child", in relation to any proceedings under this Part means:*
>
> *(a) any child who is living with or might reasonably be expected to live with either party to the proceedings;*
>
> *(b) any child in relation to whom an order under the Adoption Act 1976, the Adoption and Children Act 2002 or the Children Act 1989 is in question in the proceedings; and*
>
> *(c) any other child whose interests the court considers relevant.'*

In terms of jurisdiction, the answer is found in a judgment of Lord Justice MacFarlane in Re T (A Child)[66] where his lordship summarised the powers of the inherent jurisdiction in the context of non-molestation proceedings:

> *38. 'Firstly, there is no room for doubt that the court had jurisdiction to consider granting a non-molestation order for the protection of the child in this case under FLA 1996, s.42(2)(b). The court was seized of validly constituted 'family proceedings' (s.63(1)), namely the local authority application under the inherent jurisdiction. I do not share the judge's sense of reticence in relying upon the existence of those proceedings as a jurisdictional platform for considering granting a non-molestation order under s.42(2)(b). The application under the inherent jurisdiction had been properly made in order to achieve substantive relief in the form of an injunction to protect the child, the foster carers and their immediate environment. Permission to bring that application had been granted by HHJ Parry under CA 1989, s.100 and both that judge and HHJ Furness had granted wide-ranging injunctions under the inherent jurisdiction. The inherent jurisdiction*

66 [2017] EWCA Civ 1889

application was not some empty procedural tree, the fruit of which was to be discarded as soon as the looked-for non-molestation order had been secured. The inherent jurisdiction injunction was fixed by the judge to run for the child's minority and there is no reason why it would have been, or should have been, discharged or superseded if a non-molestation order had also been imposed.

39. *Looked at on a wider basis, it must be the case that, for s.42(2)(b) to operate, there will always be some other application in 'family proceedings' before the court, on the back of which the court will have jurisdiction to consider making a non-molestation order for the benefit of a child even if there has been no formal application made for one under FLA 1996. The provision in s.42(2)(b) is there to supplement the jurisdiction of the court in other family proceedings (for example under the Matrimonial Causes Act 1973 or the Adoption and Children Act 2002) where, because the non-molestation jurisdiction is confined to the 1996 Act, there is no other power to make a non-molestation order backed up with the criminal sanction now contained in s.42A(1). In contrast to the approach of the judge, therefore, I do not regard this as a rather strange result; on the contrary, this would appear to be the result to which s. 42(2)(b) is targeted so that, as here, where a non-molestation order may be justified, the court has jurisdiction to grant it for the protection of a 'relevant child'.*

40. *The importance of s.42(2)(b) within the structure of FLA 1996 is not to be understated. There are two separate jurisdictional avenues by which the court may make a non-molestation order. Firstly, under s.42(2)(a) which is limited to cases where an application for a non-molestation order has been made by 'a person who is associated with the respondent'; this provision is therefore very largely limited to adult relationships and it is not expressly focussed upon the protection of any relevant child. Secondly, and separately, there is the wider jurisdiction to protect 'any other party to the proceedings or any relevant child' under s.42(2)(b). The*

purpose of s.42(2)(b) would seem to be clear; it is the means by which the court may make orders for the protection of children whose circumstances have come to the notice of the court in other family proceedings.

41. *In the present case, the local authority's aim was to achieve the protection of the child and her carers from the worrying and troublesome actions of the mother and Mr JM. Once it was accepted that any order under the inherent jurisdiction could not be supported by a power of arrest, it was a perfectly legitimate step for the local authority to ask the court to consider granting a non-molestation order under the 1996 Act by utilising the jurisdiction provided by s.42(2)(b) which is designed precisely for the purpose of supplementing the court's jurisdiction in other 'family proceedings' in this way.'*

The above judgment and analyses is helpful for practitioners in understanding the jurisdictional basis for such orders when seeking to invoke the inherent jurisdiction.

Other Injunctive Provisions for the local authority

Putting aside the issue of non-molestation orders, the local may seek injunctive provisions to protect children. For example, in Birmingham City Council v Sarfraz Riaz and Others[67], Keehan J made a wide-ranging injunctive provision to prevent child sexual exploitation against 10 individuals. As Keehan J stated in the judgment at paragraph 7:

'accordingly the local authority decided to take a bold and novel step, namely, to apply for civil injunctions under the inherent jurisdiction of the High Court. The injunctive orders sought to prevent any further

67 [2014] EWHC 4247 (Fam)

contact or association with AB or with any female under the age of 18 years, previously unknown to them, in a public place'

The terms of the injunction were specified in the judgment, reading as follows:

'From the time this order is served upon X until the date specified in this order X Must Not:

a. contact AB by any means, in person and or through any third person whether by way of face to face contact, telephone (mobile/landline/facetime/skype etc.), text messages, MSM, blackberry, chatrooms, or other social media whether or not such contact is invited in the first instance by AB

b. seek the company or be in the company of AB whether or not invited to do so in the first instance by AB

c. approach AB in any manner, whether in public, on the street or other public areas such as parks, in private addresses open to certain members of the public such as any food outlet, retail outlet, café, public house, bar, hotel, club, nightclub etc, on public transport, in or at any premises associated with a sporting or entertainment activity or in any private residence, whether or not invited to do so in the first instance by AB

d. follow AB in any location public or private

e. approach any female, under the age of 18 years, not previously associated with him on a public highway, common land, wasteland, parkland, playing field, public transport stop/station.

f. pass on details for AB for example name, location, address, telephone numbers at which she can be reached or the names of other persons through whom she can be contacted save as directed by the police or order of the Court.

g. incite, encourage or facilitate the introduction of AB to any other male.

h. incite or encourage any other male to seek any form of contact with AB

i. cause, permit or allow AB or other female previously unknown to him and who may be under the age of 18 years to enter into or remain in any private motor car or taxi in which he is driving or travelling as a passenger'

The above demonstrated how wide-ranging injunctive powers can be through the inherent jurisdiction.

In any event, a local authority or a party to proceedings where an injunction has bene made pursuant to the inherent jurisdiction must ensure the important procedural points are undertaken to ensure enforceability and that they are not appealable. Namely:

A. If it is made without notice, a note of the hearing must be served with the order when the order is served;

B. Provision for the variation / discharge of the order must be made clear and who the application needs to be on notice to; and

C. The relevant wording and penal notices in the order, on the face of the order;

D. That the person who is injuncted should obtain legal advice / representation; and

E. A clear outline of the rights of the person who is subjected to the injunction, including the right to an interpreter and to request the order being translated.

Injunctions – Safety

Ordinarily, non-molestation orders and occupation orders are governed by statute, namely the Family Law Act 1996. A party can pursue an application in the local family court. At times, due to the wide-ranging powers of the inherent jurisdiction, a party may seek to apply for a powerful injunction in the High Court. Again, any application must be supported by evidence. Providing a case law example of this is Sir Nicholas Wall in CW & Ors v TW[68] who had '*made an order banning TW from the County of Wiltshire save for specified purposes.*'

It is likely many applications for injunctions have been made in the High Court through the inherent jurisdiction. The difficulty is that a lot of this immediate relief is sought on a without notice basis initially until the fuller facts are determined, or they are applied for on a very urgent basis with risk factors being identified. Judges, namely the urgent applications judge have to make quick decisive action. Consequently, there are not many reported cases dealing with the issue. But the inherent jurisdiction is wide-ranging and it is impossible an applicant apply for a wide-ranging injunctive order in emergency situations in the High Court.

Conclusion

Whilst Tipstaff orders are very powerful, they are limited in the sense of the circumstances where they may be of use, for example child abduction or to prevent a child abduction. There may be many other circumstances where an injunction is required in the High Court and through the inherent jurisdiction. This chapter outlines that there have been numerous reported cases dealing with injunctive provisions and the ability to make them under the inherent jurisdiction. In circumstances where statute may not apply, such as the Family Law Act 1996 or if the injunction is required to be wide-ranging, the inherent jurisdiction is the mechanism to make an application. This does not detract from the

68 [2011] EWHC 76 (Fam)

essential need to evidence the need of the injunction and the necessity and proportionality of it.

CHAPTER SEVEN

THE INHERENT JURISDICTION AND PRIVATE LAW MATTERS

Introduction

This Chapter will consider the inherent jurisdiction in cases where there is a private law dispute between parents and not necessarily any state involvement. Ordinarily, the inherent jurisdiction in private law disputes is rare in nature, but do exist. However, it must be outlined that many private law disputes relating to the Children Act 1989 may be heard in the High Court. This does not mean the inherent jurisdiction is being utilised, all it means is there is a level of complexity proceedings may be heard by a High Court judge.

Allocation

Proceedings do not always stay in the High Court. Eventually a case may get to a stage where the inherent jurisdiction is no longer required. For example, a child has been abducted which resulting in proceedings in the High Court. Eventually, the child may be returned. Upon this happening, the issue is, do proceedings need to stay in the High Court? Alternatively, proceedings may have commenced in the High Court or allocated up to the High Court due to a specific issue relating to the inherent jurisdiction. Once this has been achieved, the query is going to be whether proceedings should stay in the High Court or not. The issue is the guidance as outlined in the earlier chapter, but also other points relating to the case. For example, has there been a fact-finding hearing? If so, judicial continuity may be important. In a lot of cases nonetheless, as soon as the inherent jurisdiction is exhausted, for example a tipstaff order is no longer required, or a child has returned to England, a High Court judge will expect to be addressed on allocation.

In the event proceedings are reallocated down to the Family Court level, practitioners should embark upon some preparation work to ensure a swift allocation. This includes ascertaining which local court should be hearing the matter. In most cases, this is simple because a local authority could be involved, highlighting the area of the case. Or in private law proceedings, wherever the child is based. In some difficult cases, where the location of the child / parent is to be prohibited from being revealed to the other side, the court should be addressed about this issue. Equally, the High Court judge may speak to the local Designated Family Judge ['DFJ'] of the court to ascertain the best way to allocate the proceedings back down. For example, it could go to Gatekeeping or the DFJ to allocate. Further, practitioners should think about the level of judge, whether it would be appropriate to be allocated down to circuit or district judge level and this should be recorded on the face of the order.

Fact-finding hearings justifying orders under the inherent jurisdiction

In this book, there has been consideration of the role of the inherent jurisdiction in international child abduction disputes. As a consequence of child abduction or the risk of abduction, a parent or a local authority for example can apply for various orders in the inherent jurisdiction. Moving proceedings on somewhat, ultimately the court will need to determine welfare. This can include child arrangements orders in terms of Section 8 of the Children Act 1989. For example, upon findings being made and / or a welfare assessment, the next steps is to make final orders. Proceedings cannot go on forever.

In circumstances where the inherent jurisdiction has been utilised, it is likely that there may need to be a fact-finding in respect of this. For example, if a child has been wrongfully removed or retained in another country, but the respondent denies it is wrongful, the court will need to determine the facts. The same with when a child is returned back to England, what were the circumstances? Equally, if a local authority seeks an injunction or obtained an injunction or a Tipstaff order for example, does any risk arise still? These questions go to the issue as to whether there needs to be any further orders and if so, for what duration. Taking another example, if a child has been wrongfully removed but then returns to England, the applicant may say there is a real risk there may be another abduction in the future and therefore should the Tipstaff order remain? These are all important points and examples that practitioners should think about. The factual matrix often needs to be determined before any welfare assessment or before any final orders can be made.

Taking an example, in cases relating to abandonment / stranded spouses, Hogg J's guidance in Re S[69] explicitly stated that:

> '*At an early stage the court should consider whether there should be an urgent fact-finding hearing to investigate and ascertain the circumstances in which the parent and child/children came to be stranded internationally. Consideration should be given to any disputed allegations made by the stranded parent, as to the gravity of such allegation and if proved, the impact it may have upon the court's determining the welfare issues and future upbringing of the child/children concerned. If a fact-finding hearing is thought to be appropriate, directions should be given for an early hearing, and thereafter the judgment to be disclosed to Cafcass, and such other agencies including the local authority and local police as may be deemed appropriate*'

The same can be said for any other order made under the inherent jurisdiction. Given the wide-ranging effect of such an order, eventually the court will need a factual matrix in existence to consider whether to continue or discharge an order. In circumstances where a continuation is sought, the question will be for how long.

69 [2011] 1 FLR 320, para 4

A further example of the necessity and the types of questions that can be considered in cases relating to the inherent jurisdiction, particularly in proceedings relating to wardship and child abduction can be found in the 2023 authority of Morgan J in R v P[70]. In this case, her ladyship was tasked with determining the following:

> *'1) on what factual basis the children travelled to Iraq in 2018;*
>
> *(2) whilst in Iraq, why the children remained there until 2022;*
>
> *(3) what were the circumstances that caused the mother to be separated from the children; and (4) who retains their travel documents and passports'*

Upon making the relevant findings, the issue of allocation emerged. It is important to note, in general family proceedings relating to private law disputes, if there is to be a fact-finding hearing pursuant to PD12J, then the judge hearing that fact-finding needs to retain the case up to welfare. The difference in the High Court in inherent jurisdiction matters is that sometimes, as the above cases demonstrate, the court is only ascertaining certain factors relating to the orders already made. Morgan J's decision in R v P summarises this proposition because at the end of the judgment and after findings where made, her ladyship stated:

> *'...which progresses the matter to its next welfare stage, which I think we all agree is the Central Family Court. It may be that there will be other matters relating to the cross-allegations of Domestic abuse, which will be ones which will have to be considered further by any other judge, but I would be surprised if there was the need for any further issues of fact to be determined, because it seems to me, on the basis of the CAFCASS enquiries carried out thus far, that this is squarely now a matter for welfare decisions'*

70 [2023] EWCH 914 (Fam), paragraph 16

Accordingly, from the above, the next stage is welfare and that was to be determined by the local family court together with other issues relating to domestic abuse.

Turning onto fact-finding hearings generally, there is a significant amount of case law in respect of the necessity of one, enshrined further by PD12J and various authorities in the Court of Appeal. To summarise the approach, in K v K[71] the Court of Appeal. At paragraph 66 of that judgment, the Master of the Rolls says:

> *'the main things that the Court should consider in deciding whether to order a fact-finding hearing are: (a) the nature of the allegations and the extent to which those allegations are likely to be relevant to the making of the child arrangements order, (b) that the purpose of fact-finding is to allow assessment of the risk to the child and the impact of any abuse on the child, (c) whether fact-finding is necessary or whether other evidence suffices, and (d) whether fact-finding is proportionate'*

Children As a Party

In private disputes between parents in the High Court, if the inherent jurisdiction is being utilised then practitioners must have regard to the trajectory of the case. In the sense, what is the ultimate goal of the proceedings? If the inherent jurisdiction is being utilised for particular purposes, eventually a final order may need to be made. As outlined earlier in this chapter, a fact-finding hearing may be necessary. Also, practitioners must also consider having children joined to proceedings if required. It can be assumed in circumstances where proceedings are remaining in the High Court there is an element of complexity in existence. Notwithstanding this, the test and approach is within the Family Procedure Rules.

To start with, PD16A, 7.1 outlines:

71 [2022] EWCA Civ 468

"*Making the child a party to the proceedings is a step that will be taken only in cases which involve an issue of significant difficulty and consequently will occur in only a minority of cases. Before taking the decision to make the child a party, consideration should be given to whether an alternative route might be preferable, such as asking an officer of the Service or a Welsh family proceedings officer to carry out further work or by making a referral to social services or, possibly, by obtaining expert evidence*".

In terms of the test to be applied, practitioners should consider the checklist at PD16A, 7.2:

'*7.2*

The decision to make the child a party will always be exclusively that of the court, made in the light of the facts and circumstances of the particular case. The following are offered, solely by way of guidance, as circumstances which may justify the making of such an order –

(a) where an officer of the Service or Welsh family proceedings officer has notified the court that in the opinion of that officer the child should be made a party;

(b) where the child has a standpoint or interest which is inconsistent with or incapable of being represented by any of the adult parties;

(c) where there is an intractable dispute over residence or contact, including where all contact has ceased, or where there is irrational but implacable hostility to contact or where the child may be suffering harm associated with the contact dispute;

(d) where the views and wishes of the child cannot be adequately met by a report to the court;

(e) where an older child is opposing a proposed course of action;

(f) where there are complex medical or mental health issues to be determined or there are other unusually complex issues that necessitate separate representation of the child;

(g) where there are international complications outside child abduction, in particular where it may be necessary for there to be discussions with overseas authorities or a foreign court;

(h) where there are serious allegations of physical, sexual or other abuse in relation to the child or there are allegations of domestic violence not capable of being resolved with the help of an officer of the Service or Welsh family proceedings officer;

(i) where the proceedings concern more than one child and the welfare of the children is in conflict or one child is in a particularly disadvantaged position;

(j) where there is a contested issue about scientific testing'

Points (b), (c), (g) and (h) are common features that can arise in High Court private disputes arising out of proceedings where the inherent jurisdiction has or continues to be exercised. In such circumstances it is very likely the question of appointing a guardian will be an early consideration.

Conclusion

Private law disputes relate to disputes between to parents about the welfare of the subject child / children. Normal private law disputes hearing in the family court never warrant any orders under the inherent jurisdiction. This is because the issues might be complex, but not to a level where the inherent jurisdiction is needed. In many disputes in the High Court, the fact proceedings are in the High Court is because an order made under the inherent jurisdiction has been made. The original orders could have bene made without notice for a particular purpose, for example to bring a child back to England who has been unlawfully retained / removed from England. Alternatively, whatever orders made under the inherent jurisdiction may be subject to challenge. For example, the discontinuation of a tipstaff order such as a passport order. In these circumstances, proceedings may stay in the High Court as this chapter outlines. The issue of the risk factors together with the welfare checklist will have to be considered, perhaps through a fact-finding process. Practitioners should, in line with the level of complexity that exists consider to timetable proceedings in a proportionate manner and have regard to a number of issues such as the need for a fact-finding hearing, what ought to be considered at a fact-finding hearing and the appointment of a guardian.

CHAPTER EIGHT

THE INHERENT JURISDICTION AND MEDICAL TREATMENT

Introduction

The inherent jurisdiction can be utilised for vulnerable adults. This book is concerned with children only. At times, the inherent jurisdiction can be utilised and invoked for the most urgent medical treatment cases, as this book will consider.

Medical Treatment

To exercise the inherent jurisdiction, there is no limit in that only a parent or a local authority can seek relief. Taking an example, a Hospital Trust can also seek relief. The High Court is often dealing with urgent medical treatment issues where a Hospital Trust seeks a declaration in respect of an action, they wish to take concerning a child, where those with parental responsibility do not agree. The reason being, that a child is someone under the age of 16. By virtue of section 8 of the Family Law Reform Act 1969 a child has to be 16 before he or she can validly consent to a surgical procedure. In Re W (A Minor) (Consent to Medical Treatment) [72]Lord Donaldson MR stated the following:

> *'Section 8 of the Family Law Reform Act 1969 gives minors who have attained the age of 16 a right to consent to surgical, medical or dental treatment. Such consent cannot be overridden by those with parental responsibility for the minor. It can, however, be overridden by the*

[72] [1993] 1 FLR 1, page 14–16

court. This statutory right does not extend to consent to the donation of blood or organs.

A minor of any age who is 'Gillick-competent' in the context of particular treatments has a right to consent to that treatment which again cannot be overridden by those with parental responsibility, but can be overridden by the court. Unlike the statutory right this common law right extends to the donation of blood or organs.

No minor of whatever age has power by refusing consent to treatment to override a consent to treatment by someone who has parental responsibility for the minor and a fortiori a consent by the court. Nevertheless, such a refusal is a very important consideration in making clinical judgments and for parents and the court in deciding whether themselves to give consent. Its importance increases with the age and maturity of the minor.'

Therefore, when the court is faced with a child and those with parental responsibility do not agree to treatment, what is the court to do? Through case law, 10 propositions were created by Holman J in a leading case of The NHS Trust v A (a child) & Ors[73]. At paragraph 10 of the judgment, his lordship set out the following:

'i. As a dispute has arisen between the treating doctors and the parents, and one .... [party has] asked the court to make a decision, it is the role and duty of the court to do so and to exercise its own independent and objective judgment.

ii. The right and power of the court to do so only arises because the patient, in this case because [she] is a child, lacks the capacity to make a decision for [herself].

iii. I am <u>not</u> deciding what decision I might make for myself if I was, hypothetically, in the situation of the patient; nor for a child of my own

[73] [2007] EWHC 1696 (Fam)

if in that situation; nor whether the respective decisions of the doctors on the one hand or the parents on the other are reasonable decisions.

iv. The matter must be decided by the application of an objective approach or test.

v. That test is the best interests of the patient. Best interests are used in the widest sense and include every kind of consideration capable of impacting on the decision. These include, non-exhaustively, medical, emotional, sensory (pleasure, pain and suffering) and instinctive (the human instinct to survive) considerations.

vi. It is impossible to weigh such considerations mathematically, but the court must do the best it can to balance all the conflicting considerations in a particular case and see where the final balance of the best interests lies.

vii. Considerable weight (Lord Donaldson of Lymington MR referred to "a very strong presumption") must be attached to the prolongation of life because the individual human instinct and desire to survive is strong and must be presumed to be strong in the patient. But it is not absolute, nor necessarily decisive; and may be outweighed if the pleasures and the quality of life are sufficiently small and the pain and suffering or other burdens of living are sufficiently great.

viii. These considerations remain well expressed in the words as relatively long ago now as 1991 of Lord Donaldson of Lymington in Re J (A minor) (wardship: medical treatment) [1991] Fam 33 at page 46 where he said:

"There is without doubt a very strong presumption in favour of a course of action which will prolong life, but … it is not irrebuttable … Account has to be taken of the pain and suffering and quality of life which the child will experience if life is prolonged. Account has also to be taken of the pain and suffering involved in the proposed treatment… We know that the instinct and desire for survival is very

strong. We all believe in and assert the sanctity of human life .... Even very severely handicapped people find a quality of life rewarding which to the unhandicapped may seem manifestly intolerable. People have an amazing adaptability. But in the end there will be cases in which the answer must be that it is not in the interests of the child to subject it to treatment which will cause it increased suffering and produce no commensurate benefit, giving the fullest possible weight to the child's, and mankind's desire to survive."

ix. All these cases are very fact specific, i.e. they depend entirely on the facts of the individual case.

x. The views and opinions of both the doctors <u>and</u> the parents must be carefully considered. Where, as in this case, the parents spend a great deal of time with their child, their views may have particular value because they know the patient and how he reacts so well; although the court needs to be mindful that the views of any parents may, very understandably, be coloured by their own emotion or sentiment. It is important to stress that the reference is to the views and opinions of the parents. Their own wishes, however understandable in human terms, are wholly irrelevant to consideration of the objective best interests of the child save to the extent in any given case that they may illuminate the quality and value <u>to the child</u> of the child/parent relationship.'

In practice, where the above criteria were applied, the case of Re JM (A Child)[74]. In this case, the NHS Trust sought urgent permission to perform urgent surgery on a child aged 10. His lordship concluded at paragraph 10:

'In this case I have no doubt at all that the proposed procedure is in J's interest. I reach this conclusion bringing into the judicial evaluation exercise all of the matters I have mentioned above, as well as every detail of the written and oral evidence of Dr X. I give full weight to

74 [2015] EWHC 2832

> *the wishes of J as well as those of his parents. It is a strong thing for me, a stranger, to disagree with and override the wishes of J and his parents. But I have absolutely no doubt that J must be given the chance, a very good chance, of a long and fulfilling life rather than suffering, quite soon, a ghastly, agonising, death'*

Accordingly, the above demonstrates that when a court is tasked to deal with urgent issues, there needs to be medical evidence which will be considered and analysed with the other evidence generally, as Holman J indicated.

One matter practitioners should note is that these types of cases often attract media attention. Accordingly, the media are often in attendance. A Mostyn J concluded in his judgment of Re JM, he provides guidance on the approach in respect of the media at paragraph 29:

> *'In my opinion the application should be heard in private under FPR rule 27.10 but the press should be encouraged to attend under rule 27.11 and an order should be made allowing them to see the core documents under rule 29.12(1). Section 97(2) of the Children Act 1989 will prevent the child being identified and this may be bolstered by making a reporting restriction order (as I did in this case on 25 September 2015)'*.

An important distinction therefore arises in that the proceedings are not in 'open court' they are in 'private'.

Mostyn J also in Re JM considered the inherent jurisdiction and the alternative of applying for a specific issue order under the Children Act 1989. He considered the authorities in the matter and ultimately concluded the following at paragraph 27:

> *'Therefore it seems to me that if the relief sought includes final binding declarations (which will normally be the case) then the application should be framed as a combination of an application for a specific issue order (seeking the necessary leave under section 10(2)(b)) and an*

> *application for declaratory relief under the inherent jurisdiction. This will allow the application to be issued directly in the High Court where it will be listed by the Clerk of the Rules before a full time High Court Judge'*

Therefore a benefit of such complicates cases is that they will automatically be heard by a High Court Judge.

<u>End of Life Treatment</u>

There can also be the unfortunate and very distressing cases where the issue of end of life support for a child has to be considered. These cases concern the Right to Life under Article 2 of the European Convention of Human Rights. Re Y (No 1)[75] further reiterated that the right to life under Art 2 of the ECHR imposes a positive obligation to provide life sustaining treatment, but this must also be balanced in respect of responsible medical opinion is of the view that the treatment would not be in the best interests of the patient concerned[76].

In the family law context within the High Court, MacDonald J once stated[77]

> *'Where, as in this grave and difficult case, a dispute arises between parents and treating doctors regarding the proper course of treatment for a seriously ill child, the court may grant a declaration declaring that treatment in accordance with the recommendation of the child's doctors can take place, on the grounds that it is in the child's best interests (see Re B (A Minor)(Wardship: Medical Treatment) (1982) 3 FLR 117). The jurisdiction of the court to make such an order arises where a child lacks the capacity to make the decision for him or herself, in the context of a disagreement between those with parental*

75 [2015] EWHC 1920 (Fam), para 37

76 See also R (Burke) v The General Medical Council [2005] EWCA 1003

77 King's College Hospital NHS Foundation Trust v T, L, I, para 1:

> *responsibility for the child and those treating the child (An NHS Trust v MB [2006] EWHC 507 (Fam)). The court has no power to require doctors to carry out a medical procedure against their own professional judgment'*

As the above judgment outlines as does many others considering the issue, the judgments deal with a vast amount of medical evidence and submissions on the issue as to the child's best interests. This can be summarised in the following case law principles:

In Yates and Gard v Great Ormond Street Hospital for Children NHS Foundation Trust[78] McFarlane LJ stated that:

> *'As the authorities to which I have already made reference underline again and again, the sole principle is that the best interests of the child must prevail and that must apply even to cases where parents, for the best of motives, hold on to some alternative view'*

In terms of considering the competing interests and focusing on the welfare, Baroness Hale in Aintree University Hospital NHS Trust v James[79] stated:

> *'[22] Hence the focus is on whether it is in the patient's best interests to give the treatment rather than whether it is in his best interests to withhold or withdraw it. If the treatment is not in his best interests, the court will not be able to give its consent on his behalf and it will follow that it will be lawful to withhold or withdraw it. Indeed, it will follow that it will not be lawful to give it. It also follows that (provided of course they have acted reasonably*

78 [2017] EWCA Cv 410

79 [2013] UKSC 67

and without negligence) the clinical team will not be in breach of any duty toward the patient if they withhold or withdraw it."

and

"[39] The most that can be said, therefore, is that in considering the best interests of this particular patient at this particular time, decision-makers must look at his welfare in the widest sense, not just medical but social and psychological; they must consider the nature of the medical treatment in question, what it involves and its prospects of success; they must consider what the outcome of that treatment for the patient is likely to be; they must try and put themselves in the place of the individual patient and ask what his attitude towards the treatment is or would be likely to be; and they must consult others who are looking after him or are interested in his welfare, in particular for their view of what his attitude would be.'

Other Medical Disputes – Vaccinations

An area which has formulated in many reported cases in the recent years is the issue of vaccinations. This was particularly apparent amidst the covid-19 pandemic. A useful case dealing with this is a judgment of Hayden J in Re T[80]. Paragraph 1 of the case introduced the issue as: *'This is an application made by the applicant Local Authority for a declaration that it is in the interests of T (a 10-month-old child) to receive a schedule of vaccinations, conveniently set out in the report of Dr Neil Douglas. Dr Douglas specialises in community paediatrics and is responsible for Looked-After Children ('LAC') in the relevant NHS Trust'*

This case was following a final care order being made by the judge following contested public law proceedings. As such, the local authority

80 [2020[EWHC 220 (Fam).

was involved and therefore the applicant to the proceedings as the subject child was in foster care, as paragraph 2 outlines.

Before turning to the decision of Re T, there is a vast amount of case law dealing with vaccinations in the High Court following public law proceedings. For example,

In Re SL (Permission to vaccinate)[81], MacDonald J outlined the legal principles as:

> '*33. In this case the court is concerned with the issue of vaccinations in the context of children who are the subject of care orders and thus the dispute is between the local authority sharing parental responsibility for the child and the parent with parental responsibility. In the circumstances where SL is in the care of the local authority, by virtue of s 9(1) of the Children Act 1989 the local authority cannot apply for a specific issue order with respect to the issue of vaccination. Further, given the gravity of the issue in dispute, it is not appropriate for the local authority simply to give its consent to immunisation pursuant to the provisions of s 33(3) of the Children Act 1989 on the basis of its shared parental responsibility for SL under the interim care order (see A Local Authority v SB, AB & MB) [2010] 2 FLR 1203 and Re Jake (Withholding Medical Treatment) [2015] EWHC 2442 (Fam)).*'

In terms of the local authority bringing the matter to the court arena when there are issues of parental responsibility following a care order, Munby P in Re AB[82] stated:

> '*Whatever its strict rights may be, a local authority will usually be ill advised to rely upon its parental responsibility under section 33(3)(a) of the 1989 Act as entitling it to authorise medical treatment opposed*

81 [2017] EWHC 125 (Fam)

82 [2013] EWFC 2, at paragraph 24 (iii)

by parents who also have parental responsibility: see Barnet London Borough Council v AL and others [2017] EWHC 125 (Fam), [2017] 4 WLR 53, para 32, and the discussion in Re C (Children: Power to Choose Forenames) [2016] EWCA Civ 374, [2017] 1 FLR 487, paras 92-95.'

In terms of the jurisdictional arguments relating to the issue, King LJ in Re C (Children)[83] referred in respect of declaration and the scope of the inherent jurisdiction the following:

'*90. Whilst I may not necessarily agree with the precise way that jurisdictional issues have been approached or expressed in these very difficult cases, what is clear is that there is a cohort of cases where the common theme is that a party (whether it be a local authority or, often, an NHS Trust) has sought to bring an issue before the court, believing it to be of too great a magnitude to be determined without the guidance of the court, and without all those with parental responsibility having an opportunity to express their view as a part of the decision making process.*

91. Most commonly, examples are found in the so called 'medical treatment' cases where, either an NHS Trust seeks a declaration from the court that they would not be acting unlawfully in pursuing or desisting from a form of treatment notwithstanding the parent's refusal to consent, or alternatively, a local authority seeks to invoke the inherent jurisdiction of the court and thereby to submit to the court's jurisdiction notwithstanding that care proceedings may have been open to them.'

Turning back to Re T and Hayden J, his case is of particular importance because it considers the jurisdictional issues in play and in particular,

83 [2016] EWCA Civ 374

whether the local authority can have recourse to the statutory provisions. Namely,

Section 33(3) Children Act 1989 states:

(1) Where a care order is made with respect to a child it shall be the duty of the local authority designated by the order to receive the child into their care and to keep him in their care while the order remains in force. […]

(3) While a care order is in force with respect to a child, the local authority designated by the order shall–

(a) have parental responsibility for the child; and

(b) have the power (subject to the following provisions of this section) to determine the extent to which

(i) a parent, guardian or special guardian of the child; or (ii) a person who by virtue of section 4A has parental responsibility for the child, may meet his parental responsibility for him.

(4) The authority may not exercise the power in subsection (3)(b) unless they are satisfied that it is necessary to do so in order to safeguard or promote the child's welfare.

[…]'

The above, should be read alongside the duties of a local authority, set out at Section 22 of the Act:

'*(3) It shall be the duty of a local authority looking after any child–*

(a) to safeguard and promote his welfare; and

(b) to make such use of services available for children cared for by their own parents as appears to the authority reasonable in his case. […]

(4) Before making any decision with respect to a child whom they are looking after, or proposing to look after, a local authority shall, so far as is reasonably practicable, ascertain the wishes and feelings of–

(a) the child;

(b) his parents;

(c) any person who is not a parent of his but who has parental responsibility for him; and

(d) any other person whose wishes and feelings the authority consider to be relevant, regarding the matter to be decided

(5) In making any such decision a local authority shall give due consideration–

(a) having regard to his age and understanding, to such wishes and feelings of the child as they have been able to ascertain;

(b) to such wishes and feelings of any person mentioned in subsection (4)(b) to (d) as they have been able to ascertain; and

(c) to the child's religious persuasion, racial origin and cultural and linguistic background.'

Hayden J envisaged the situation where a parent may themselves seek an application under the inherent jurisdiction to stop such vaccinations. Nonetheless, Hayden J's judgment provides clarity in respect of the duties of the local authority and their powers in respect of parental responsibility. His lordship summarised the position at paragraphs 16 and 17 as follows:

'I have no doubt at all that if the Local Authority had signalled its intention to have T vaccinated under the authority of s.33(3) CA, this would have led to an immediate application on behalf of the parents to invoke the inherent jurisdiction. Nonetheless, I, for my part, can see

> *no reason why what are ultimately routine vaccinations should not fall within the scope of the interventions contemplated by s.33(3) CA. Indeed it strikes me as disproportionate to expect a Local Authority to be required to apply to a High Court Judge to initiate proceedings, the result of which has been in every reported case to authorise vaccination.*
>
> *In this application, as in every application of its kind, the Local Authority has been required to commission an immunisation report. This has been undertaken by Dr Douglas, who has been responsible for assessing T in the course of the LAC adoption medical process, and who has had overall responsibility for T's health throughout his life. T has been subject to interim and now final care orders since birth and is considered by Dr Douglas to be in good health. For reasons that will emerge below, it is important to record that Dr Douglas has considered T's medical records, most recently in preparation for the adoption medical'*

In terms of the ultimate order and the balance between both provisions, his lordship stated at paragraph 35:

> *'For the reasons that I have analysed above, I consider that this question of immunisation properly falls within the Local Authority's remit, as prescribed by s.33(3) CA. However, given that it comes before me as a contested application for a declaration under the inherent jurisdiction, I am prepared to grant the declaration sought by the Local Authority. I take this approach because I am entirely satisfied that had the Local Authority signalled that they intended to pursue the schedule of immunisation under s.33(3) CA, this would have been met by an immediate application on behalf of the parents for a declaration that such a course would be unlawful. Thus, the inherent jurisdiction would have been triggered in any event'*

Conclusion

As this chapter considers, the inherent jurisdiction is a tool that can be utilised in the most extreme cases relating to medical treatment. This can commence from a local authority, a hospital trust or even a parent. A declaration can be sought to make something lawful, where there is an issue of consent in relation to parental responsibility. Practitioners must note the particular procedures that arise in this area of the law, namely the interest in the media and the issue of reporting restrictions. Further, in terms of other treatments such as vaccinations where the local authority is involved, practitioners working within the local authority must consider and obtain advice as early as possible as to whether what treatment they seek falls within the statutory provisions or whether they have no choice but to seek a declaration in the High Court.

CHAPTER NINE

CONCLUDING THOUGHTS

This book demonstrates that the inherent jurisdiction is a vastly important mechanism which can be utilised in England and Wales. It is a unique power that has an important role to play in terms of justice. A parent, a local authority, an interested party can seek the relief of the High Court if required. Notwithstanding this, a benefit of the inherent jurisdiction proceedings is that they are heard by High Court judges who are experienced and dealing with tricky issues on a daily basis. Often, the inherent jurisdiction is utilised in an urgent manner because of a serious issue has arisen. This could be in respect of medical treatment or child abduction. Once the inherent jurisdiction is used, the trajectory of the case can lead to many different outcomes. Practitioners must always have in mind the relief that is being sought, why and once given, if there is any further role of the inherent jurisdiction. If there is, then issues relating to ascertaining the factual matrix for a fact-finding hearing for example must be considered.

Statute cannot cover every scenario relating to children and this is why the inherent jurisdiction is vitally important. Transparency in family proceedings is vitally important. The more cases that are published then greater clarity will arise in respect of the types of cases the inherent jurisdiction can be used and for what purpose.

MORE BOOKS BY LAW BRIEF PUBLISHING

A selection of our other titles available now:-

'A Practical Guide to Estate Administration and Crypto Assets' by Richard Marshall
'A Practical Guide to Managing GDPR Data Subject Access Requests – Second Edition' by Patrick O'Kane
'A Practical Guide to Parental Alienation in Private and Public Law Children Cases' by Sam King QC & Frankie Shama
'Contested Heritage – Removing Art from Land and Historic Buildings' by Richard Harwood QC, Catherine Dobson, David Sawtell
'The Limits of Separate Legal Personality: When Those Running a Company Can Be Held Personally Liable for Losses Caused to Third Parties Outside of the Company' by Dr Mike Wilkinson
'A Practical Guide to Transgender Law' by Robin Moira White & Nicola Newbegin
'A Practical Guide to 'Stranded Spouses' in Family Law' by Mani Singh Basi
'A Practical Guide to Residential Freehold Conveyancing' by Lorraine Richardson
'A Practical Guide to Pensions on Divorce for Lawyers' by Bryan Scant
'A Practical Guide to Challenging Sham Marriage Allegations in Immigration Law' by Priya Solanki
'A Practical Guide to Legal Rights in Scotland' by Sarah-Jane Macdonald
'A Practical Guide to New Build Conveyancing' by Paul Sams & Rebecca East
'A Practical Guide to Defending Barristers in Disciplinary Cases' by Marc Beaumont
'A Practical Guide to Inherited Wealth on Divorce' by Hayley Trim
'A Practical Guide to Practice Direction 12J and Domestic Abuse in Private Law Children Proceedings' by Rebecca Cross & Malvika Jaganmohan
'A Practical Guide to Confiscation and Restraint' by Narita Bahra QC, John Carl Townsend, David Winch
'A Practical Guide to the Law of Forests in Scotland' by Philip Buchan
'A Practical Guide to Health and Medical Cases in Immigration Law' by Rebecca Chapman & Miranda Butler

'A Practical Guide to Bad Character Evidence for Criminal Practitioners by Aparna Rao

'A Practical Guide to Extradition Law post-Brexit' by Myles Grandison et al

'A Practical Guide to Hoarding and Mental Health for Housing Lawyers' by Rachel Coyle

'A Practical Guide to Psychiatric Claims in Personal Injury – 2nd Edition' by Liam Ryan

'Stephens on Contractual Indemnities' by Richard Stephens

'A Practical Guide to the EU Succession Regulation' by Richard Frimston

'A Practical Guide to Solicitor and Client Costs – 2nd Edition' by Robin Dunne

'Constructive Dismissal – Practice Pointers and Principles' by Benjimin Burgher

'A Practical Guide to Religion and Belief Discrimination Claims in the Workplace' by Kashif Ali

'A Practical Guide to the Law of Medical Treatment Decisions' by Ben Troke

'Fundamental Dishonesty and QOCS in Personal Injury Proceedings: Law and Practice' by Jake Rowley

'A Practical Guide to the Law in Relation to School Exclusions' by Charlotte Hadfield & Alice de Coverley

'A Practical Guide to Divorce for the Silver Separators' by Karin Walker

'The Right to be Forgotten – The Law and Practical Issues' by Melissa Stock

'A Practical Guide to Planning Law and Rights of Way in National Parks, the Broads and AONBs' by James Maurici QC, James Neill et al

'A Practical Guide to Election Law' by Tom Tabori

'A Practical Guide to the Law in Relation to Surrogacy' by Andrew Powell

'A Practical Guide to Claims Arising from Fatal Accidents – 2nd Edition' by James Patience

'A Practical Guide to the Ownership of Employee Inventions – From Entitlement to Compensation' by James Tumbridge & Ashley Roughton

'A Practical Guide to Asbestos Claims' by Jonathan Owen & Gareth McAloon

'A Practical Guide to Stamp Duty Land Tax in England and Northern Ireland' by Suzanne O'Hara

'A Practical Guide to the Law of Farming Partnerships' by Philip Whitcomb

'Covid-19, Homeworking and the Law – The Essential Guide to Employment and GDPR Issues' by Forbes Solicitors

'Covid-19 and Criminal Law – The Essential Guide' by Ramya Nagesh

'Covid-19 and Family Law in England and Wales – The Essential Guide' by Safda Mahmood
'A Practical Guide to the Law of Unlawful Eviction and Harassment – 2nd Edition' by Stephanie Lovegrove
'Covid-19, Brexit and the Law of Commercial Leases – The Essential Guide' by Mark Shelton
'A Practical Guide to Costs in Personal Injury Claims – 2nd Edition' by Matthew Hoe
'A Practical Guide to the General Data Protection Regulation (GDPR) – 2nd Edition' by Keith Markham
'Ellis on Credit Hire – Sixth Edition' by Aidan Ellis & Tim Kevan
'A Practical Guide to Working with Litigants in Person and McKenzie Friends in Family Cases' by Stuart Barlow
'Protecting Unregistered Brands: A Practical Guide to the Law of Passing Off' by Lorna Brazell
'A Practical Guide to Secondary Liability and Joint Enterprise Post-Jogee' by Joanne Cecil & James Mehigan
'A Practical Guide to the Pre-Action RTA Claims Protocol for Personal Injury Lawyers' by Antonia Ford
'A Practical Guide to Neighbour Disputes and the Law' by Alexander Walsh
'A Practical Guide to Forfeiture of Leases' by Mark Shelton
'A Practical Guide to Coercive Control for Legal Practitioners and Victims' by Rachel Horman
'Tackling Disclosure in the Criminal Courts – A Practitioner's Guide' by Narita Bahra QC & Don Ramble
'A Practical Guide to the Law of Driverless Cars – Second Edition' by Alex Glassbrook, Emma Northey & Scarlett Milligan
'A Practical Guide to TOLATA Claims' by Greg Williams
'A Practical Guide to Elderly Law – 2nd Edition' by Justin Patten
'A Practical Guide to Responding to Housing Disrepair and Unfitness Claims' by Iain Wightwick
'A Practical Guide to the Law of Bullying and Harassment in the Workplace' by Philip Hyland
'How to Be a Freelance Solicitor: A Practical Guide to the SRA-Regulated Freelance Solicitor Model' by Paul Bennett
'A Practical Guide to Prison Injury Claims' by Malcolm Johnson

‘A Practical Guide to the Small Claims Track – 2nd Edition’ by Dominic Bright
‘A Practical Guide to Advising Clients at the Police Station’ by Colin Stephen McKeown-Beaumont
‘A Practical Guide to Antisocial Behaviour Injunctions’ by Iain Wightwick
‘Practical Mediation: A Guide for Mediators, Advocates, Advisers, Lawyers, and Students in Civil, Commercial, Business, Property, Workplace, and Employment Cases’ by Jonathan Dingle with John Sephton
‘The Mini-Pupillage Workbook’ by David Boyle
‘A Practical Guide to Crofting Law’ by Brian Inkster
‘A Practical Guide to the Law of Domain Names and Cybersquatting’ by Andrew Clemson
‘A Practical Guide to the Law of Gender Pay Gap Reporting’ by Harini Iyengar
‘NHS Whistleblowing and the Law’ by Joseph England
‘Employment Law and the Gig Economy’ by Nigel Mackay & Annie Powell
‘A Practical Guide to Noise Induced Hearing Loss (NIHL) Claims’ by Andrew Mckie, Ian Skeate, Gareth McAloon
‘An Introduction to Beauty Negligence Claims – A Practical Guide for the Personal Injury Practitioner’ by Greg Almond
‘Intercompany Agreements for Transfer Pricing Compliance’ by Paul Sutton
‘Zen and the Art of Mediation’ by Martin Plowman
‘A Practical Guide to the SRA Principles, Individual and Law Firm Codes of Conduct 2019 – What Every Law Firm Needs to Know’ by Paul Bennett
‘A Practical Guide to Adoption for Family Lawyers’ by Graham Pegg
‘A Practical Guide to Industrial Disease Claims’ by Andrew Mckie & Ian Skeate
‘A Practical Guide to Redundancy’ by Philip Hyland
‘A Practical Guide to Vicarious Liability’ by Mariel Irvine
‘A Practical Guide to Applications for Landlord’s Consent and Variation of Leases’ by Mark Shelton
‘A Practical Guide to Relief from Sanctions Post-Mitchell and Denton’ by Peter Causton
‘A Practical Guide to Equity Release for Advisors’ by Paul Sams
‘A Practical Guide to Financial Services Claims’ by Chris Hegarty
‘The Law of Houses in Multiple Occupation: A Practical Guide to HMO Proceedings’ by Julian Hunt

'Occupiers, Highways and Defective Premises Claims: A Practical Guide Post-Jackson – 2nd Edition' by Andrew Mckie
'A Practical Guide to Financial Ombudsman Service Claims' by Adam Temple & Robert Scrivenor
'A Practical Guide to Running Housing Disrepair and Cavity Wall Claims: 2nd Edition' by Andrew Mckie & Ian Skeate
'A Practical Guide to Holiday Sickness Claims – 2nd Edition' by Andrew Mckie & Ian Skeate
'Arguments and Tactics for Personal Injury and Clinical Negligence Claims' by Dorian Williams
'A Practical Guide to Drone Law' by Rufus Ballaster, Andrew Firman, Eleanor Clot
'A Practical Guide to Compliance for Personal Injury Firms Working With Claims Management Companies' by Paul Bennett
'RTA Allegations of Fraud in a Post-Jackson Era: The Handbook – 2nd Edition' by Andrew Mckie
'RTA Personal Injury Claims: A Practical Guide Post-Jackson' by Andrew Mckie
'On Experts: CPR35 for Lawyers and Experts' by David Boyle
'An Introduction to Personal Injury Law' by David Boyle

These books and more are available to order online direct from the publisher at www.lawbriefpublishing.com, where you can also read free sample chapters. For any queries, contact us on 0844 587 2383 or mail@lawbriefpublishing.com.

Our books are also usually in stock at www.amazon.co.uk with free next day delivery for Prime members, and at good legal bookshops such as Wildy & Sons.

We are regularly launching new books in our series of practical day-to-day practitioners' guides. Visit our website and join our free newsletter to be kept informed and to receive special offers, free chapters, etc.

You can also follow us on Twitter at www.twitter.com/lawbriefpub.

www.ingramcontent.com/pod-product-compliance
Lightning Source LLC
LaVergne TN
LVHW022055200926
848481LV00003B/918
9781916698208